DRAGONS

DRAGONS

FEARSOME MONSTERS
— FROM —
MYTH AND FICTION

GERRIE McCALL & KIERON CONNOLLY

SCHOLASTIC

www.scholastic.com

This edition published by Scholastic Inc., 557 Broadway, New York, NY 10012 by arrangement with Amber Books Ltd.

Scholastic Canada Ltd.
Markham, Ontario

Grolier International, Inc.
Makati City, Philippines

1 2 3 4 5 6 7 8 9 10

ISBN: 978-0-545-62726-9

Editorial and design by
Amber Books Ltd
74–77 White Lion Street
London N1 9PF
United Kingdom
www.amberbooks.co.uk

Project Editor: Michael Spilling
Design: Andrew Easton

Printed in Shenzhen, China

Contents

Introduction

Dragons have been with us for a very long time. One of the oldest stories in the world, more than 3,000 years old, is the Mesopotamian story of Marduk defeating the dragon Tiamat. Dragons also appeared in ancient Greek mythology and the Bible tells of evil seven-headed dragons. In China, emperors were even said to have been descended from dragons.

A guardian of treasure, a nuisance, a creator, or a destroyer—dragons can be many things, different cultures giving them different characters. In China, they are usually good, powerful, and are often gods. In European folklore, dragons are mostly evil and terrorize people. Chinese dragons do not have wings and are more like a snake, but can still fly, while European dragons are a mix of a reptile and a bird and can breathe fire.

But why have we ever imagined there are such things as dragons? For some cultures, dragon stories are about explaining the creation of the world, such as the story of Marduk and Tiamat, where the dragon is the monster that causes chaos and must be defeated. After this, the earth can be separated from the heavens and the land from the sea. For the ancient Greeks, dragons were monstrous and sometimes gods, but for Christians in Europe, dragons became evil and man had to defeat them.

Creating dragons was also a way of explaining the unknown, such as why the sun rises in the east or why the moon changes appearance each month. And it was only in the last 200 years that we understood from fossils what the dinosaurs were. Before then, some people thought dinosaur bones probably belonged to fabulous, huge beasts—dragons.

Whether one-headed or seven-headed, swimming or flying, sleeping or sleepless, gods or demons, there have been many different kinds of dragons and they still seem to capture our imagination. Here be dragons!

Beowulf's Dragon

WINGS
Batlike wings attached to the torso by robust muscles lift the dragon in flight. The bones within the wing structure are hollow to reduce their weight.

TAIL
The barbed tail shaped like an arrowhead can be used as a weapon in battle. In flight, the tail operates like a rudder, balancing the dragon and allowing it to execute skillful aerial maneuvers.

EYES
Adapted to see in the dim light of caves, the dragon's eyes are well suited for watching over its hoard of plundered treasure.

JAWS
Its fiery breath lights the skies. Chain mail provides no defense against its crushing jaws and venomous fangs. A reservoir of venom is located in the upper jaw.

BODY
The dragon's enormous body is blackened by the soot of its own flames. Its blue-green scales glow with inner fire.

Coiled in a cavern beneath a gray rock there is a terrifying dragon—a firedrake measuring 50 feet (15 m) long. The dragon guards a lair filled with piles of priceless treasure. Its heavy body blocks daylight from reaching the armor, goblets, jewels, coins, and golden swords it hoards deep in the cave. When a thief steals a golden cup from its lair, the dragon rampages through the countryside, burning everything it sees. The firedrake breathes flames that light up the sky, terrifying villagers and burning every home in Geatland. Beowulf, King of the Geats, armed with a magic sword, leads an army into battle to face the dragon.

6 ft
(1.8 m)

SIZE COMPARISON

▶ BEOWULF STRIKES THE DRAGON WITH HIS SWORD, but the blow glances off the beast's terrible hide. Beowulf is engulfed in dragon flames, a sight so terrifying that his army flees. Only the faithful Wiglaf remains to help. Beowulf breaks off the blade of his magic sword in the dragon's head. Bitten on the neck by the dragon, Beowulf is soaked in his own blood but continues fighting. Wiglaf stabs the dragon in a vulnerable place and Beowulf slashes it through the middle, cutting the monster in two and ending its life.

Where in the world?

Geatland, a region in the south of Sweden, is where Beowulf met the mighty dragon in battle. Geatland's deep forests provided the ideal habitat for a firedrake.

● SWEDEN

Did you know?

● Beowulf dies from his battle wounds. The dragon's treasure is removed from the cave and buried with Beowulf. All the pieces of the dragon's corpse are thrown into the sea.

● The dragon's flames are so intense that they burn Wiglaf's shield down to its handle. Wooden shields, such as the one Wiglaf used, are a poor choice when doing battle with a firedrake.

● Beowulf carries an iron shield bearing the image of a dragon.

● A dragon's lightweight bones are tougher than reinforced concrete.

● Smoke rising from the mouth of a cave is usually a tell-tale sign that a dragon resides within.

● The dragon is the largest known flying creature in mythology.

Gorynych *(GOH-ri-nitch)*

HEADS
Three fanged, fire-spitting heads with terrible horns make it impossible to approach Gorynych. Six watchful eyes and a heightened sense of smell enable him to detect a maiden from a mile (1.6 km) away.

BODY
The scaly body produces a reek of sulfur that hangs around Gorynych like a sinister cloud.

CLAWS
Iron claws rip knights' suits of armor open as if they were aluminum cans.

WINGS
Although his great bulk prevents him from flying quickly, Gorynych's wings allow him to descend in places where he is least expected.

TAILS
Seven wildly thrashing tails render the dragon's back end as hazardous as his front.

This savage Russian dragon has three fire-spitting heads and seven tails. Gorynych walks on his two hind legs and has two small front legs like a Tyrannosaurus rex. His iron claws can slash through any shield or suit of armor. The air around Gorynych reeks of sulfur, a sign of evil. His uncle, the sorcerer Nemal Chelovek, kidnaps the czar's daughter and intends her to wed Gorynych. The princess is imprisoned in the sorcerer's dark mountain castle. Desperate to have his daughter back, the czar offers a huge reward to anyone who can rescue the princess from the castle. Many princes try and fail.

6 ft
(1.8 m)

SIZE COMPARISON

▶ IVAN, A PALACE GUARD who understands the speech of animals, overhears two crows discussing where the princess is hidden. The czar gives Ivan a magic sword to help him on his rescue mission. Nemal Chelovek's fortress is unguarded because he believes no one would dare approach him. Nemal Chelovek turns himself into a giant when he discovers Ivan in his castle. The magic sword flies from Ivan's hands, killing the giant, then flies through the castle halls until it finds and slays Gorynych. Ivan marries the princess.

Where in the world?

The fearsome seven-tailed Gorynych is featured in folktales and myths originating from Russia and Ukraine.

● RUSSIA

● UKRAINE

Did you know?

● Gorynych caused eclipses of the sun and moon. The fact that they reappeared showed that even a powerful dragon could not defeat the sun and moon. The Russians took this as a sign that dragons can be defeated by the righteous.

● Not all Slavic dragons are destructive. The Slovenian city of Ljubljana is protected by a dragon. This benevolent dragon is pictured on the city's coat of arms.

● Dragon blood is so venomous that soil does not absorb it.

● There are no cave paintings of dragons because caves are a favorite residence of these creatures. The dragon residing in the cave would have driven all cave painters away.

● A magic sword that enables the warrior to stand far away from the dragon is the ideal weapon to defeat these terrible beasts.

Krak's Dragon

TAIL
The swishing tail knocks over fences, damages bridge supports, and strips bark from trees. It can also crush a human's rib cage with a single blow.

HEAD
The dragon's massive skull is counterbalanced in flight by its long tail. Its piercing vision allows it to spot its next meal from half a mile (0.8 km) away.

WINGS
Broad wings enable airborne attacks, which are the most effective method of terrorizing the countryside.

JAWS
Terrible, fire-belching jaws are lined with pointed fangs. The dragon's scorching breath destroys barns, forests, public buildings, and flocks of sheep.

CLAWS
Hooked claws shred and dig into the flesh of the dragon's helpless prey as it holds its squirming meal in its toothy jaws.

In Polish legend, a fearsome dragon lives in a dark cave at the foot of Wawel Hill along the banks of the Vistula River. Every day it rages through the countryside, terrifying the inhabitants of Kraków. The bad-tempered, fire-breathing dragon eats farm animals and people. Anything that runs from it is fair game. After it gobbles down several small children, it plunders homes for prized possessions to take back to its cave. Many bold knights try to slay this dragon and perish in flame for their efforts. Its daily thefts begin to affect the local economy. The people of the area grow poorer and the princess worries she will never marry.

6 ft
(1.8 m)

SIZE COMPARISON

▶ KRAK, A PEASANT BOY employed as a shoemaker's apprentice, is intelligent, cunning, and possessed of special cooking skills. The king is desperate for anyone's dragon-slaying services and allows the raggedly dressed boy to try. Krak stuffs three roasted sheep full of sulfur and hot spices and leaves the spicy meal next to the dragon's cave. The greedy dragon gulps them down whole. The spices and sulfur burn the dragon's stomach. It drinks half the Vistula River to quench its thirst. Its swollen, burning gut bursts and the dragon dies.

Where in the world?

Every citizen of Poland is familiar with the stories of the death, trauma, and destruction caused by Krak's dragon.

● POLAND

Did you know?

● The city of Kraków is named after the heroic Krak.

● Near the cavern beneath the castle of Kraków, there is a monument to Krak's dragon. The statue of the dragon has been rigged with a natural-gas nozzle so that it breathes fire every few minutes.

● Krak marries the princess and is given the dragon's hoarded treasure. After the death of the king, Krak ascends the throne.

● Many dragons prefer to sleep on top of a pile of jewels and treasure because more traditional bedding materials are too easily ignited by their fiery breath.

● Trickery is often the preferred method for defeating the most dangerous dragons. Cunning is generally a mightier weapon than a sword when facing a beast of such tremendous size, aggression, and appetite.

Knucker

EYES
Eerie eyes glow with
a chemical that allows
the Knucker to see
great distances in the
densest waters and
the darkest forests.

TAIL
The dragon's
gigantic tail is so
powerful it can
swat down trees.

WINGS
Small wings allow the
Knucker to fly low
through marshy areas in
search of likely victims.
When in water, the
wings act as fins.

JAWS
Immense jaws open wide
enough to swallow a horse
and cart whole. Teeth larger
than railroad spikes line
a mouth that reeks of the
Knucker's nauseating breath.

BODY
A streamlined, eel-shaped body aids
the Knucker in navigating quickly
and silently through the chilly waters
of the knuckerhole.

A terrible, water-dwelling dragon, the Knucker makes nightly raids on Lyminster farms for meals of horses and cows. Any person crossing its path is just another meal to the Knucker. The dragon squeezes its prey to death or shreds its victim's flesh to ribbons with its venomous fangs. The thrashing of the Knucker's immense tail topples the trees in Batworth Park. Many a still night in Lyminster is shattered by the hiss and roar of the ravenous dragon. So many villagers and farm animals go missing that the mayor offers a reward to anyone who can kill the Knucker and allow the villagers to live without fear.

6 ft
(1.8 m)

SIZE COMPARISON

▶ JIM, A FARMER'S BOY FROM A NEARBY VILLAGE, tells the mayor his plan to defeat the Knucker. The mayor orders the villagers to help Jim with everything he needs. The villagers give Jim all the ingredients for an enormous pie. Jim bakes a pie laced with poison for the Knucker. He hauls the huge pie out to the knuckerhole using a borrowed cart and horse. The Knucker eats the pie, horse, and cart. The poison kills the dreaded dragon and Jim chops off its head with an ax.

Where in the world?

The Knucker rises from the knuckerhole in Lyminster, West Sussex, in southern England. Its residence, the knuckerhole, is a bottomless pool fed by an underground spring.

● ENGLAND

Did you know?

● St. Mary Magdalene Church in Lyminster contains the Slayer's Slab, a gravestone dedicated to the hero who killed the Knucker.

● The British explorer Sir Francis Drake was called "The Dragon" by the Spanish because he was a fierce warrior and he helped defeat the Spanish Armada.

● The knuckerhole where the Knucker lives is a bottomless pool that neither freezes in winter nor dries up in summer. Six bell ropes from Lyminster Church were tied together and let down in the knuckerhole to measure its depth, but the bottom was never found.

● Residents of Lyminster once used water from the knuckerhole as a cure-all tonic.

● The county of Sussex once had a thriving dragon population. Bignor Hill and St. Leonard's Forest in Sussex also have a history of dragon infestations.

Orochi *(oh-ROH-chee)*

TAILS
Eight muscly tails create strange whistling noises as Orochi thrashes them in anger.

EYES
Eight sets of eyes that are as red as winter cherries keep watch in all directions.

BELLY
Perpetually bloody and inflamed from his kills, the ravenous dragon's belly must always be filled.

BODY
The giant body stretches over eight valleys and eight hills. Orochi's back is covered with moss and trees.

Each year the evil dragon Orochi demands that a Japanese maiden be offered to him in sacrifice. Even the bravest of warriors cannot defeat this vicious, cunning beast. His gigantic body slithers across eight hills and valleys, and his eight hungry heads make him impossible to approach. One day Susanoo, the god of the sea and storms, comes upon two weeping parents. Seven of their daughters have been devoured by Orochi in the past seven years. Now their eighth and only remaining daughter is to be sacrificed to Orochi. Susanoo agrees to slay the dragon if their eighth daughter will be his wife.

6 ft
(1.8 m)

SIZE COMPARISON

▶ SUSANOO TRANSFORMS THE MAIDEN into a comb, which he safely hides in his hair. Susanoo arranges eight enormous vats of rice wine in a circle and leaves them out to tempt the dragon. Attracted by the smell of the strong wine, Orochi plunges each of his eight heads into a vat and drinks greedily. The drunken dragon collapses helpless to the ground and Susanoo uses his powerful sword to slice Orochi to pieces. The local river runs red with the blood of the slain menace.

Where in the world?

Orochi's eight hungry heads terrorized the citizens of Izumo Province in Japan near the foot of Mount Sentsuzan.

JAPAN

Did you know?

• As Susanoo hacks up Orochi, he discovers a sacred sword embedded in one of his tails.

• The dragon's full name, Yamata no Orochi, means "big snake of eight branches."

• Fresh maidens are a favorite meal of dragons worldwide.

• During the Edo period (1603–1868), it was popular for Japanese firefighters to get dragon tattoos. They believed the image of the dragon would protect them while fighting fires.

• Although fearsome and powerful, Japanese dragons are also fair and benevolent. The Japanese believe dragons bring wealth and good luck.

• Images of dragons adorn many Buddhist temples in Japan. Dragons are thought to dispel evil.

St. George and the Dragon

TAIL
A flick of this dragon's razor-sharp tail leaves a man with bloodied stumps where he once had limbs.

HEAD
The solid, thick skull contains eyes with extra optic nerves for keen vision and nostrils that belch foul black fumes.

WINGS
Wing bones attached to the broad back by a system of mighty muscles lift the heavy beast into the air.

NECK
An elongated neck keeps the dragon's fire-breathing ability at a safe distance from its own body.

BODY
Scales like steel plates on the dragon's body shatter St. George's spear when he first attempts to stab the creature.

CLAWS
Sturdy talons leave telltale gouges in the ground wherever the dragon walks.

This bloodthirsty dragon lives by a spring that provides all the water for the city of Cyrene. Whenever the citizens of Cyrene want water, they are faced with the immense beast. Unhappy with the diet of sheep the citizens feed it, the dragon demands human sacrifices. A human sacrifice has to be given to the dragon daily before it allows anyone to draw water from the spring. The only fair way to determine the daily victim is by drawing lots. The princess is chosen as the next victim and her father, the king, is distraught. He offers the citizens all his riches if they will spare his daughter, but the citizens refuse.

6 ft
(1.8 m)

SIZE COMPARISON

▶ THE PRINCESS IS TIED TO A WOODEN STAKE near the spring. St. George, a soldier of the Roman Empire, discovers the distressed princess and unties her. St. George charges the dragon on horseback. His sturdy lance penetrates deep enough only to wound the foul creature. Using the princess's sash as a leash, St. George and the princess lead the injured dragon into town. St. George announces he will finish off the dragon if the citizens convert to Christianity. They agree to convert and St. George draws his sword and kills the beast.

Where in the world?

This dragon nests at a spring that provides water for the people of Cyrene, Libya, in northern Africa.

●LIBYA

Did you know?

● St. George is the patron saint of England, knights, archers, and butchers.

● The flag of Wales bears the image of a red dragon. It is believed to be the oldest national flag still in use.

● Hundreds of years ago, dinosaur fossils were believed to be dragon bones.

● Dragoon soldiers carried a musket called the dragon. The musket was given this name because it emitted flames when fired.

● The various parts of the dragon are believed to have magical properties. Anyone eating dragon's heart would be able to understand the speech of birds. Eating dragon's tongue gives one the power to win any argument. Dragon's blood provides protection against injury from swords.

Balaur

EYES
Although the princess is beautiful, it is not her looks that attract Balaur but that she is the most desired girl in the village.

HEADS
Balaur has three serpent-shaped heads.

VOICE
Although he has the body of a dragon, Balaur speaks like a man.

WINGS
Balaur does not stay in the same cave all the time; he flies to different parts of Romania. Often the first time people know about Balaur is when he descends from the clouds and bites them.

GEMSTONE
By dribbling saliva, Balaur could make precious gemstones. These the villagers exchanged for the finest robes.

Fat-Frumos, a handsome young knight, arrives in a village in the forest. Although it is not a wealthy village, all the people are dressed in the finest robes. Weeping and begging, they plead with Fat-Frumos for his help. They explain that, by dribbling saliva, Balaur made many precious stones for them, which they exchanged for beautiful robes. They were very grateful, but while the riches distracted them, Balaur seized their princess and took her prisoner. Fat-Frumos agrees to help the villagers if they will give up their robes and stones and follow his plan.

6 ft
(1.8 m)

SIZE COMPARISON

► THAT NIGHT, A MONSTER NEVER SEEN BEFORE climbs to Balaur's cave. The monster is taller and wider than the dragon; its multicolored skin sparkles. The monster calls out to Balaur, "Tell me what I am and no harm will come to you." Balaur has no idea what this fiend is. In fact, the villagers have sewn together their robes and gems, which they propped up with tree branches, to create the monster. Balaur tries to look more closely at the monster, but Fat-Frumos jumps out and drives his sword into Balaur's belly. The dragon collapses, and Fat-Frumos rescues the princess.

Where in the world?

Balaur is from Romania in southeastern Europe. The vampire Dracula comes from a region of Romania called Transylvania.

ROMANIA

Did you know?

• The villagers later use Balaur's bones to build a barn, and Fat-Frumos marries the princess.

• In one tale, Fat-Frumos chops a head off Balaur when it surfaces from a lake. Fat-Frumos thinks he has defeated the dragon, but another head appears. Fat-Frumos cuts that head off, too. But again, another head appears. Balaur turns out to be a twelve-headed dragon. Fat-Frumos cuts all the heads off. In doing this, Fat-Frumos saves a griffin's chicks that Balaur was trying to eat.

• Later, when the villagers hear of dragons offering precious stones, they are not tempted to accept them.

Wyvern *(WY-vurn)*

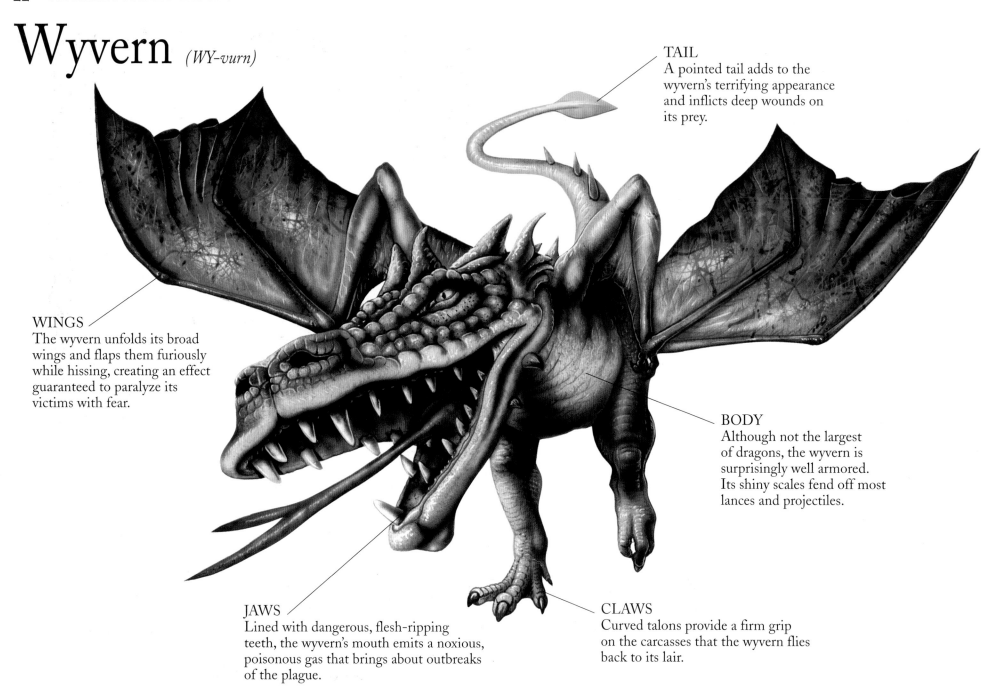

TAIL
A pointed tail adds to the wyvern's terrifying appearance and inflicts deep wounds on its prey.

WINGS
The wyvern unfolds its broad wings and flaps them furiously while hissing, creating an effect guaranteed to paralyze its victims with fear.

BODY
Although not the largest of dragons, the wyvern is surprisingly well armored. Its shiny scales fend off most lances and projectiles.

JAWS
Lined with dangerous, flesh-ripping teeth, the wyvern's mouth emits a noxious, poisonous gas that brings about outbreaks of the plague.

CLAWS
Curved talons provide a firm grip on the carcasses that the wyvern flies back to its lair.

The most famous wyvern is one adopted as a pet by young Maud. While walking in the woods near her home in Mordiford, Maud discovers a baby wyvern. Its body is no bigger than a cucumber and is covered in sparkling, bright-green scales. Maud takes the helpless wyvern home, but her parents forbid her to keep it. Instead of setting it free, Maud places the tiny dragon in her secret hiding place in the woods. She visits it daily, feeding it milk and playing with it. The wyvern grows rapidly and soon milk is not enough to satisfy its ravenous appetite. The wyvern begins to feast on local livestock.

6 ft
(1.8 m)

SIZE COMPARISON

▶ THE WYVERN QUICKLY DISCOVERS that farmers make better meals than farm animals. Despite its newly acquired taste for human flesh, the wyvern remains gentle with Maud. Garston, a man from one of Mordiford's best families, dons his armor and rides out to slay the wyvern. His sturdy shield protects Garston from the flame-spouting wyvern. Garston pierces the wyvern's shiny scales with his sword, fatally wounding the creature. Maud kneels on the bloodied grass beside the wyvern. Weeping, she cradles her dying friend in her arms.

Where in the world?

Wyverns were plentiful in medieval Mordiford, Herefordshire, in western England. It seemed almost anyone could stumble across one with little effort.

● ENGLAND

Did you know?

● Because of their flesh-eating habits, wyverns make unsatisfactory pets! Although they are harmless as babies, dragons' bloodthirsty instincts always set in by adulthood.

● The wyvern is associated with war, pestilence, and envy. It is believed to bring outbreaks of the plague wherever it goes.

● Its traits of strength, power, and endurance made the wyvern a popular symbol on medieval coats of arms. Its image on shields was used to strike fear into the hearts of enemies.

● British dragons have been known to inhabit places as diverse as caves, fields, woods, swamps, gullies, moors, corn stacks, water holes, and abbey ruins.

● The coat of arms of Moscow bears the image of a soldier on horseback spearing a wyvern.

Zilant

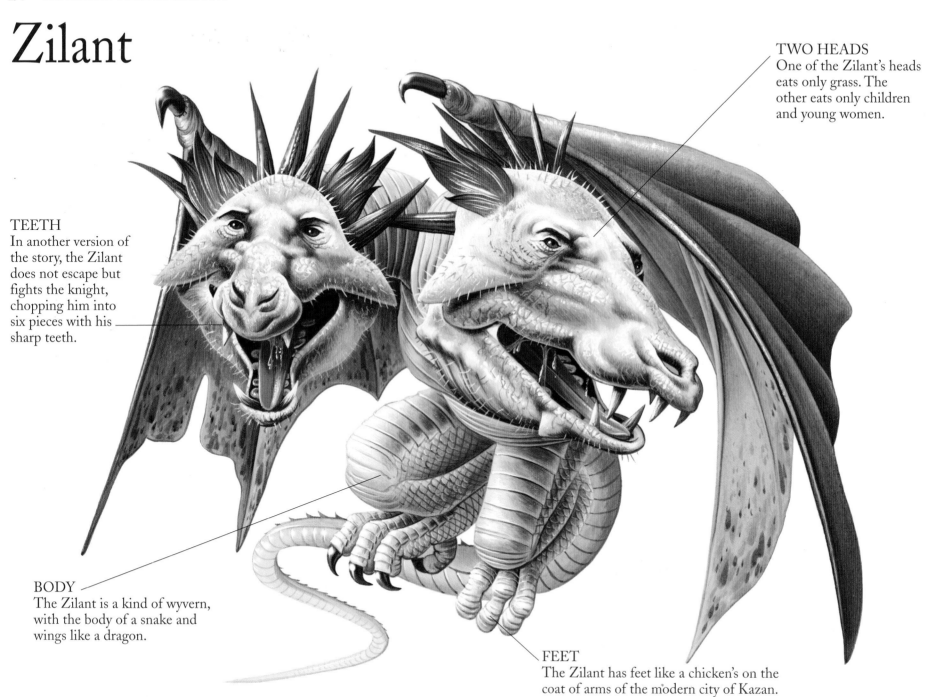

TWO HEADS
One of the Zilant's heads eats only grass. The other eats only children and young women.

TEETH
In another version of the story, the Zilant does not escape but fights the knight, chopping him into six pieces with his sharp teeth.

BODY
The Zilant is a kind of wyvern, with the body of a snake and wings like a dragon.

FEET
The Zilant has feet like a chicken's on the coat of arms of the modern city of Kazan.

In this tale from Kazan in Russia, a beautiful young woman marries a man from Kazan. She finds it a long walk to fetch water from the Kazanka River every day. She complains to the khan (the local leader) and advises him to move the city to Zilantaw Hill, which is nearer to the river. They move the city but find that Zilantaw Hill is home to many snakes as wide and long as logs.

The leader of these snakes is the giant, two-headed Zilant, who eats young women and children. Walking a long way to fetch water now seems little trouble compared to escaping the Zilant.

6 ft
(1.8 m)

SIZE COMPARISON

▶ A WIZARD ADVISES THE KHAN TO BUILD A PILE OF STRAW and wood near the hill. In spring, the snakes come out of their winter burrow and slide into the dry straw. A young knight is given the task of setting the straw on fire and burning the snakes alive. Even as the snakes burn, their foul smell kills people. However, the Zilant escapes to the nearby Kaban Lakes, where it rules the Underwater Kingdom of Kaban. Today, swimmers in the lakes can feel the bite of the Zilant, reminding them that it is still there.

Where in the world?

The Zilant comes from the city of Kazan, the capital of the Republic of Tatarstan in the Russian Federation. Kazan is 450 miles (724 km) east of Moscow.

TATARSTAN

Did you know?

● Since the eighteenth century, a one-headed version of the Zilant has been the emblem of Kazan.

● According to local legend, any snake that lives for one hundred years turns into a Zilant.

● There are many different versions of the Zilant story. One Islamic story from the region describes the Zilant as a female dragon who is about to be killed. She pleads with Allah (God) to give her wings. When her wish is granted, she flies away.

● It is possible that at one time Zilantaw Hill really was the home of many snakes. It was a high, dry island and thus would have been a likely place for snakes to hibernate in winter.

Bolla & Kulshedra

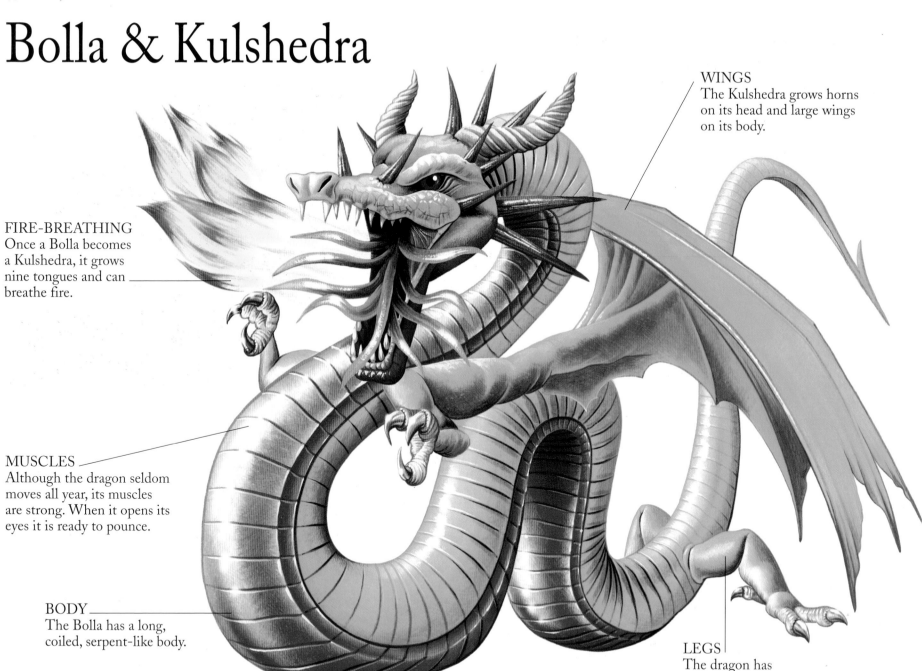

WINGS
The Kulshedra grows horns on its head and large wings on its body.

FIRE-BREATHING
Once a Bolla becomes a Kulshedra, it grows nine tongues and can breathe fire.

MUSCLES
Although the dragon seldom moves all year, its muscles are strong. When it opens its eyes it is ready to pounce.

BODY
The Bolla has a long, coiled, serpent-like body.

LEGS
The dragon has four small legs.

In Albania, Romania, and Hungary, some people believe that if a snake lives long enough and is not seen by a human, it will eventually turn into a dragon. In Albania, this dragon is called a Bolla. It keeps its eyes closed almost all year, because if it ever sees a human it has to eat the person. On St. George's Day (April 23rd), the Bolla opens its eyes and devours the first human it sees. If a Bolla lives for more than one hundred years, it transforms into a Kulshedra—a twelve-headed female dragon covered from head to toe in red hair.

6 ft
(1.8 m)

SIZE COMPARISON

▶ KULSHEDRAS CAUSE DROUGHTS, DEMAND HUMAN SACRIFICES in return for water, and cannot be defeated by a human. However, in Albania there are Draguas, semi-human men who are immensely strong and have invisible wings under their arms. Their main aim in life is to kill Kulshedras. They spend their childhood training in methods to fight these dragons. When they see a Kulshedra, they go berserk. They throw boulders, farm tools, and even uprooted trees and houses until the Kulshedra is knocked unconscious. Then, they throw the Kulshedra into a river.

Where in the world?

The Bolla comes from Albania in southeastern Europe. In some tales, the Kulshedra is thrown into the River Shkumbin in central Albania.

● ALBANIA

Did you know?

● Although many dragons are neither male nor female, Kulshedras are represented as female dragons. They can spit fire and possess the moon and the sky.

● Kulshedras can turn themselves into women as well as eels, frogs, turtles, and salamanders.

● In Albania, the word for "grass snake" is also bolla.

● Kulshedras also guard Earthly Beauty, a sorceress who lives in the underworld. Sometimes, she can be good, but she is usually an evil character.

● The children of Kulshedras are called Shlligas. They can cause storms.

Cuelebre *(KAY-leh-breh)*

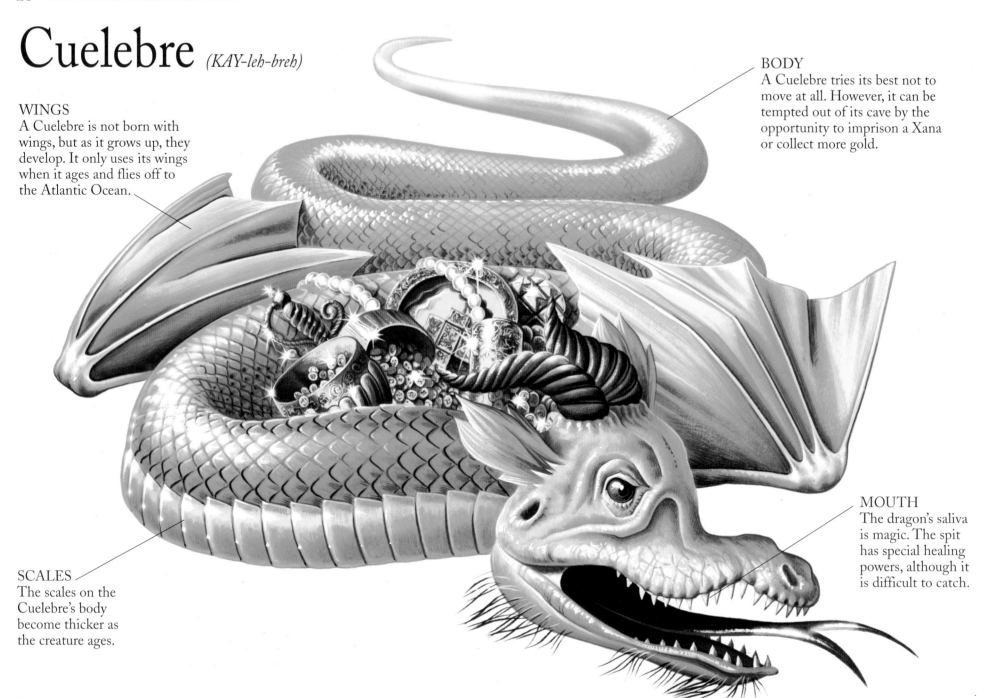

WINGS
A Cuelebre is not born with wings, but as it grows up, they develop. It only uses its wings when it ages and flies off to the Atlantic Ocean.

BODY
A Cuelebre tries its best not to move at all. However, it can be tempted out of its cave by the opportunity to imprison a Xana or collect more gold.

SCALES
The scales on the Cuelebre's body become thicker as the creature ages.

MOUTH
The dragon's saliva is magic. The spit has special healing powers, although it is difficult to catch.

Cuelebres cannot die of natural causes. They just grow older and scalier, and bat wings sprout from their bodies. They make their homes in caves and often imprison beautiful, female water spirits known as Xanas. Like many dragons, they love and guard treasure. They do not move much, but when they do, it is to eat cattle or people. Although they are dangerous, their spit turns into magic stones that can cure many diseases—but it is also impossible to grab one of these stones without being eaten by the dragon. They are not dangerous on Midsummer's Eve (the night of June 21st), the shortest night of the year.

6 ft
(1.8 m)

SIZE COMPARISON

▶ THE SOLDIER'S MOTHER IS VERY ILL. He lights a fire outside the dragon's cave, and into the flames he rolls a sparkling quartz stone. "In that fire, I've a gemstone better than your gold," the soldier tells the Cuelebre. Peering at the different-colored flames dancing around the quartz, the dragon is dazzled and begins to drool. The soldier catches the spit in his handkerchief and, lifting the quartz with some tongs, thrusts it into the Cuelebre's mouth. The dragon chokes. Hurrying home, the soldier unwraps the new magic stone in his handkerchief. He watches the color return to his mother's cheeks as she begins to heal.

Where in the world?

Cuelebres appear in the Asturian and Cantabrian mythology of northern Spain.

SPAIN

Did you know?

• The other way to kill a Cuelebre is to feed it bread filled with pins.

• Some versions of the story say that, in their old age, Cuelebres fly off to a mythical island in the Atlantic Ocean.

• In Catalonia in northeastern Spain lives a Drac, which is usually a two-legged dragon with a pair of wings and the face of a lion or a cow. Its burning breath is poisonous and rots everything.

• Apart from the Drac, there are reports of other animal-faced dragons in Europe. In 1702, a professor collected stories in Switzerland of sightings of cat-faced dragons, flammable dragons, noisy dragons, smelly dragons, feathered dragons, and bald dragons. He did not see any dragons himself, and he did not believe all the stories, but he did believe that there were dragons in the Swiss Alps.

Tugarin Zmeyevich

(too-GAH-rin ZMAY-eh-vitch)

EARS
Tugarin's ears are almost eight inches (20 cm) long.

EYES
Some stories about Tugarin say that he is so big that his eyes are at least two feet (60 centimeters) apart.

FIRE
Tugarin threatens to strangle Alyosha with smoke and scorch him with fire.

STOMACH
Tugarin's stomach is alive with many fire-breathing snakes.

There are many tales about a knight fighting a dragon, but what if the dragon itself is a knight? From a distance, Tugarin Zmeyevich might appear to be a knight—he rides a horse and he has the outline of a knight. But seen close up, his true identity becomes clear—he is huge, he hisses, his body is covered in fire-breathing snakes, and he can grow papery wings that allow him to fly. He can burn his opponents with fiery sparks and is strong enough to throw burnt logs at people. And unlike a knight, he is cruel and evil.

6 ft
(1.8 m)

SIZE COMPARISON

▶ THE YOUNG KNIGHT ALYOSHA POPOVICH visits Prince Vladimir. At dinner, Alyosha notices Tugarin Zmeyevich's brutish behavior—he pushes himself between Prince Vladimir and Vladimir's wife, he does not say his prayers, and he gobbles up much of the food. Alyosha insults Tugarin and Tugarin challenges Alyosha to a duel. Outside, Tugarin flies into the sky. He throws logs and fiery sparks at Alyosha. Alyosha prays for rain and when it pours down, Tugarin's papery wings collapse and Tugarin falls to the ground. Alyosha cuts off Tugarin's head.

Where in the world?

Tales about Tugarin Zmeyevich are found in the eastern Slavic mythology of Ukraine and Russia.

RUSSIA

UKRAINE

Did you know?

● Alyosha gives Tugarin's head to Prince Vladimir, but he scatters Tugarin's body over the field of battle.

● Besides the story of Tugarin Zmeyevich, there is also the tale of the dragon Goryschche in Russian folklore. This a huge, twelve-headed, female dragon that carries off hundreds of young Russian men to her underground den in the mountains. After many adventures, a young hero called Dobrynya Nikitich frees the men and slays the dragon.

● In Russian folklore, when dragons are approaching, eagles scream from the tops of oak trees, lightning flashes, thunder roars, and winds whip up waves on rivers and at sea.

● In all Russian folktales, dragons are close to water, fire, air, and the darker forces of nature.

● Russian dragons can be male or female.

Lindworm

EYES
In the *Hamar Chronicles* dating from about 1550, the lindworm is described as having red, burning eyes, and a mane on its vast neck.

SKIN
If someone finds the skin that a lindworm has shed, they will magically and immediately learn a great deal about nature and medicine.

SIZE
Some versions of the story say the lindworm is so big that it could coil itself around Thora's father's whole house. Also, lindworms never stop growing.

FEET
Tales differ over whether a lindworm has feet or not. Some stories describe it as a worm with no feet. Others say that it just has front claws, and some claim that it has two feet.

The Earl of Gothland in Sweden gives a baby lindworm—a small, wingless dragon—to his daughter Thora. Curled up in its casket, the lindworm looks very cute, and Thora is delighted. The lindworm grows bigger and bigger, however, until eventually it can wrap its whole body around Thora's bedroom. Then the lindworm traps Thora inside, keeping her hostage, and demands an ox for its dinner every day. The Earl promises his daughter's hand in marriage to the man who can free her from the lindworm. But can a man wearing a pair of fur pants really save her?

6 ft
(1.8 m)

SIZE COMPARISON

▶ RAGNAR HEARS ABOUT THE LINDWORM and puts on a pair of old, shaggy pants that he covers with tar and sand. Armed with a spear, he approaches the lindworm. The dragon blows poison at Ragnar's body, but the man's fur pants all covered in tar and sand protect him from the blast. When Ragnar is close enough to the lindworm, he pushes his spear into the creature's heart, killing it. He cuts off the lindworm's head and marries Thora. Thereafter, he is known as Ragnar Hairy-Pants.

Where in the world?

SWEDEN

In Gothland in southwestern Sweden, Ragnar Lodbrok ("Hairy-Pants") was a legendary Norse ruler in Scandinavia in the Viking era during the ninth century.

Did you know?

● There are sculptures of lindworms in Sweden made as early as the eleventh century.

● The people of Klagenfurt, Austria, once thought that a lindworm was responsible for flooding in the town. They caught it by tying a bull to a chain. When the lindworm ate the bull, the local people reeled the lindworm in like a fish on a hook, and the knights killed it.

● A statue of the Klagenfurt lindworm was made in 1590. The head of the statue was based on the skull of a woolly rhinoceros, which had been found in the town in 1335. This might have been the first attempt to reconstruct an extinct animal. The lindworm appears on the city's coat of arms.

Fafnir

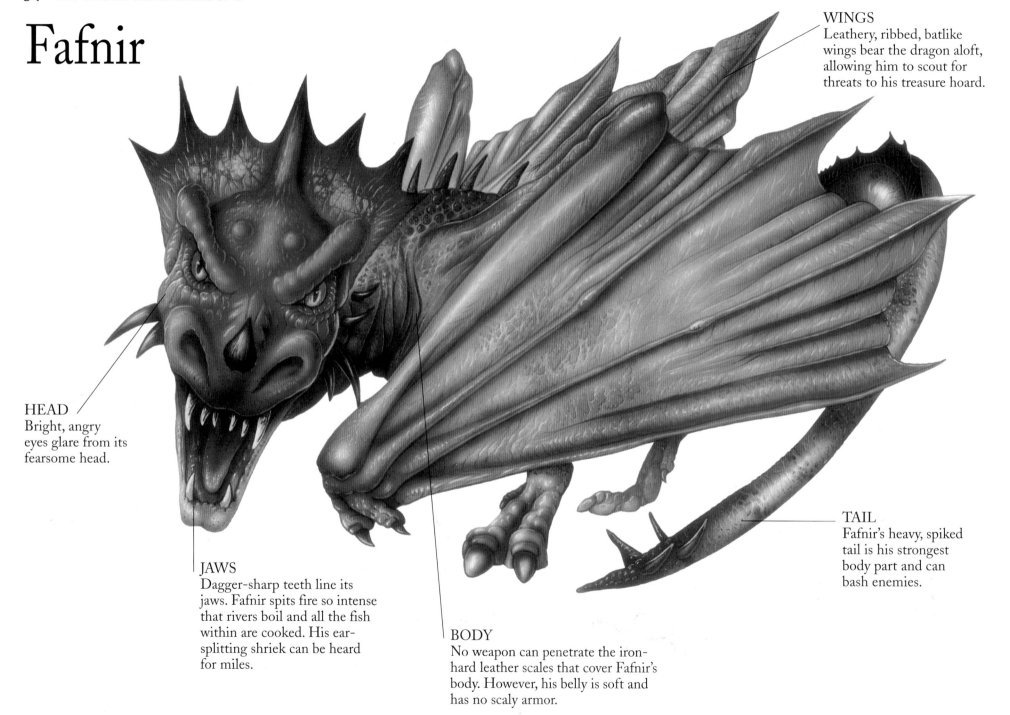

WINGS
Leathery, ribbed, batlike wings bear the dragon aloft, allowing him to scout for threats to his treasure hoard.

HEAD
Bright, angry eyes glare from its fearsome head.

JAWS
Dagger-sharp teeth line its jaws. Fafnir spits fire so intense that rivers boil and all the fish within are cooked. His ear-splitting shriek can be heard for miles.

BODY
No weapon can penetrate the iron-hard leather scales that cover Fafnir's body. However, his belly is soft and has no scaly armor.

TAIL
Fafnir's heavy, spiked tail is his strongest body part and can bash enemies.

Greed gave rise to this mighty dragon. One of a dwarf-king's three ogre sons, Fafnir covets his father's treasure. He murders his father and transforms himself into a fearsome, wicked dragon who guards all the gold. Fafnir's dragon body is covered with leather scales that are as hard as iron. No known weapon can penetrate his hide. His ridged spine ends in a spiked tail that he uses to thrash anyone who comes near his lair. He is able to boil rivers with his fiery breath until all the fish within it are cooked. Greed runs in Fafnir's family. His brother Regin covets the treasure that Fafnir stole from their father.

6 ft
(1.8 m)

SIZE COMPARISON

▶ REGIN PERSUADES BRAVE SIGURD TO SLAY THE DRAGON. Once Fafnir is dead, Regin plans to steal the treasure and kill Sigurd. Sigurd knows he cannot defeat Fafnir with brute force, so he digs a trench along the path the dragon takes. Armed with his father's sword, Sigurd hides in the trench, pulling branches and leaves over the opening so the dragon will not see him. Sigurd waits until Fafnir passes overhead and thrusts his sword into the dragon's soft belly. Fafnir dies in agony from the fatal wound.

Where in the world?

A figure from Norse mythology, Fafnir is known in the Scandinavian countries of Sweden, Denmark, and Norway.

NORWAY
SWEDEN
DENMARK

Did you know?

● Sigurd's hands are wet with the dragon's blood after the slaying. He removes Fafnir's heart to roast it on a fire so Regin can eat it. When Sigurd wipes his bloodied hand across his mouth, he accidentally tastes Fafnir's blood. The magical properties of dragon blood allow him to understand the speech of birds. The birds warn Sigurd that Regin plans to kill him and steal all the treasure.

● Regin brews a poisoned broth that he intends to use to kill Sigurd. Sigurd forces Regin to drink the poison instead.

● Keen eyesight allows Fafnir to spot the glint of a precious jewel from great distances, even in dim light.

● Richard Wagner tells the story of Fafnir in his opera *Siegfried*.

Sarkany

HEADS
A Sarkany's seven heads act independently of each other. One can be eating, another talking, another drinking, another sleeping, another shouting, another staring, and still another laughing.

EYES
A Sarkany's red-rimmed eyes can see in the dark.

WINGS
A Sarkany's wings only allow it to fly a few feet. It uses them to launch itself at prey. It is usually seen riding a horse.

SKIN
Since a Sarkany only comes out at night, its skin is ghostly pale.

The origins of the Sarkanys are unclear, but people say that they are men who once drank dragon's blood in the belief that they would gain eternal life. It did not make them immortal, but it did make them very powerful dragon-men. A Sarkany is most often seen riding through the forest just as the sun is setting and night is drawing in. He can be weakened by cutting off one of his heads, but to kill him, all seven heads need to be cut off. In Hungarian folklore, wizards called Garabonciás can tame more common dragons. But even they cannot defeat a Sarkany.

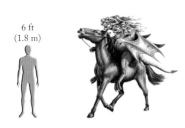

6 ft
(1.8 m)

SIZE COMPARISON

▶ IN ONE STORY, A FATHER HAS STOLEN FROM HIS VILLAGE. With his daughter Rita, he flees deep into the dark forest. They are soon lost. In a moonlit clearing, they see a figure on horseback—the seven heads of a Sarkany, all twisting in different directions. Rita gasps. One Sarkany head hears her. The other Sarkany heads turn. With her father, Rita runs back into the trees. The Sarkany gallops toward them. Rita falls, but the Sarkany rides past her. Rita hears her father's cries of agony as the Sarkany attacks him. She climbs a tree and waits for dawn.

Where in the world?

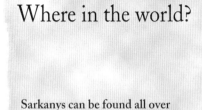

Sarkanys can be found all over Hungary in central Europe.

●HUNGARY

Did you know?

• If a Sarkany goes after someone, that person might escape if the Sarkany decides the attack is only for fun. But if the Sarkany approaches someone peacefully, then that person is doomed. It means that the Sarkany has been asked to take that person to hell.

• Sarkanys like to see people folk dancing. However, for the Sarkanys, it is a sport to make people keep dancing until they drop down dead. The different heads place bets on how long it will take for the person to collapse. The winning head gets the first bite of the dead body.

• Garabonciás can tame giant, winged dragons called Zomoks. They saddle them and ride them across the sky, hiding in storm clouds.

• Today, different kinds of dragons in Hungary are called Sárkánys.

Zahhak

HORNS
Zahhak has devil's horns. He is cunning, strong, and possessed of all possible sins. He rules with the help of demons called daevas.

SERPENTS
Two brave cooks in Zahhak's kitchen saved the lives of many men by serving sheep's brains instead of human brains to Zahhak's serpent-heads.

WINGS
Zahhak is an "azi," which means "serpent" or "dragon." With his dragon wings he flies over enemies, defeating warriors and terrifying people.

BODY
In later versions, Zahhak appears as a man with snakes growing out of his cheeks. But in earlier versions, Zahhak is a three-headed dragon.

Zahhak is the son of the ruler, but as a young man he is easily influenced by evil advisors. One persuades Zahhak to kill his father by digging a pit and covering it with leaves. His father falls in and dies, making Zahhak ruler. His advisor kisses Zahhak on both cheeks and immediately two snake heads grow out of his face.

These heads need to be fed two human brains every day. With the help of demons, Zahhak rules as a tyrant for a thousand years. It is believed that, when the world ends, he will return and kill one in three humans and animals, before he is destroyed.

6 ft
(1.8 m)

SIZE COMPARISON

▶ ZAHHAK HAD VISIONS THAT HE WAS GOING TO BE ATTACKED. He ordered his men to find and kill this attacker, but learns that it was only a nine-year-old boy, Fredon, and that Fredon had already fled. Later, Fredon leads an army against Zahhak's palace. Fredon attacks Zahhak, and snakes and scorpions burst from the wounds. But the god Ormazd tells Fredon not to kill Zahhak, because then the world would become overrun with these creatures. Instead, Fredon imprisons Zahhak in a cave beneath Mount Damavand, where he will remain until the end of time.

Where in the world?

Zahhak is found on Mount Damavand, a volcano and the highest peak in Iran.

●IRAN

Did you know?

• Tales of Zahhak, who is also known as Azhi Dahaka and Dahag, exist in Persian and Arabic folklore. The original story appears in Zoroastrian religious texts.

• A blacksmith called Kava had 18 children, but Zahhak had served 17 of them to the snakes in his cheeks. Zahhak showed mercy on the eighteenth child, who was in prison, but this still didn't make Kava a supporter of Zahhak.

• With his brother Spitiyura, Zahhak attacked Yima (Jamshid), a hero who had grown arrogant. They cut Yima in half with a saw.

• Fredon attacked Zahhak with a mace specially made from the head of an ox. In Zahhak's dream he saw three warriors attacking him, one with a mace, and then saw himself dragged off to a mountain. The other two attackers might have been Yima's daughters, Arnavaz and Shahrnavaz, whom Fredon had   ited from Zahhak's prison.

Lagarfljót Worm

(LARH-ger-floht)

TAIL
When a diver once managed to cut off its tail, the Lagarfljót monster grew another one, just like a gecko does.

FINS
Divers manage to tie the monster down by its fins and tail. But the middle of its body can still twist up and reach the water's surface.

EYES
Its large, piercing eyes can see up through the murky depths and spot a fishing boat to attack.

TEETH
Its sharp teeth bite into the legs of swimmers in the lake.

BODY
The Lagarfljót worm has a long, slithery body.

People say there is no such thing as dragons, but there are still dragons in the world—think of the bearded dragon, mountain dragon, and Komodo dragon. These are all lizards, from ones small enough to fit into the palm of a human hand to the Komodo dragon, which can grow up to ten feet (three meters) long. When animals grow so large, scientists suggest it is because there are no predators to eat them. This might just have been the case with the Lagarfljót worm. As in many dragon stories, the Lagarfljót worm began life very small but soon grew bigger and more dangerous than any human or animal around.

6 ft
(1.8 m)

SIZE COMPARISON

▶ A MOTHER GIVES HER DAUGHTER A GOLDEN RING. To make the best use of the ring, the mother tells the girl she should put it under a lindworm—a snakelike, wingless dragon. The girl catches the lindworm and places it on the ring inside her linen chest. But after a few days, the lindworm has already grown so large that it breaks open the chest. Terrified, the girl throws the chest with the ring and the lindworm into Lake Lagarfljót. There, the lindworm grows into a giant serpent, spitting poison and attacking people and animals who enter the water.

Where in the world?

ICELAND

The dragon can be found in Lake Lagarfljót in Iceland. The lake is 16 miles (26 km) long, 1.6 miles (2.6 km) wide, and 367 feet (112 m) deep.

Did you know?

• Two men from Lapland in far northern Scandinavia come to Lake Lagarfljót, but they are unable to kill the monster. All they can do is tie the serpent to the bottom of the lake.

• The story of the Lagarfljót monster was first recorded in 1345.

• Like the Loch Ness monster in Scotland, there are still occasional sightings of the Lagarfljót monster. If it is seen, it is said that there will be terrible weather and bad harvests for a year.

• Lindworm means "heath snake."

• Lake Lagarfljót is also home to Skirimsl, a giant sea monster, which is now peaceful but will one day break free and bring chaos.

Nidhogg

(NEED-hog)

HEIGHT
According to some sources, Nidhogg is taller than a multi-story building. It can rear up on its hind legs but walks on all fours.

WINGS
The dragon can fly with its enormous wings. Its five fingerlike bones are spanned by leathery skin to allow it to take to the air.

JAWS
Nidhogg's teeth are sharp and set in powerful jaws. They ooze with the juice from corpses and tree-root sap.

SCALES
Most of Nidhogg's body is covered with impressive body armor. It also has spikes on its back, tail, neck, and head, and a full set of killer claws.

Nidhogg is a mighty dragon from Norse and Germanic legend. It lives in the realm of the dead known as Niflheim or Helheim, and its name means "the tearer of corpses." Nidhogg eats the flesh of dead people, thrown down to it from Earth. It is also known to suck the blood of life's less honorable characters, such as liars, cheats, and murderers. Niflheim is a fitting home for these abominable people: it is the darkest, coldest, and lowest of the nine worlds of the dead. Nidhogg's home is a pit of venomous serpents near Hvergelmir, or "the bubbling cauldron," a spring that is the source of the world's rivers.

6 ft
(1.8 m)

SIZE COMPARISON

▶ AS A CHANGE FROM EATING DEAD FLESH and drinking blood, Nidhogg sometimes chews at the roots of Yggdrasil, the tree of life. It finally succeeds in gnawing through the roots of the tree, with the help of four serpents, but this sparks a war on Earth. After a dreadful three-year winter, the gods fight the frost giants in a monumental battle at Ragnarok. Nidhogg is involved but is not killed. Instead, the dragon survives and returns to its home, where it feasts on the many bodies thrown to it from the battlefield.

Where in the world?

Tales of Nidhogg are found in myths from many northern European countries, including Germany, Denmark, Sweden, Norway, and Iceland.

ICELAND

NORWAY

SWEDEN

DENMARK

GERMANY

Did you know?

● An eagle lives at the top of the tree of life. Nidhogg sometimes breaks from its meal of corpses to send a squirrel up the tree to torment the eagle.

● Nidhogg's name is sometimes said to mean "the dread biter," "striking full of hatred," or "evil blow."

● Some stories say that when Nidhogg entered the battle of Ragnarok, it took corpses with it to help with the fighting.

● A dragon or monster named Nidhogg appears as a character in several computer and video games, and also in a Viking LEGO set.

Tiamat

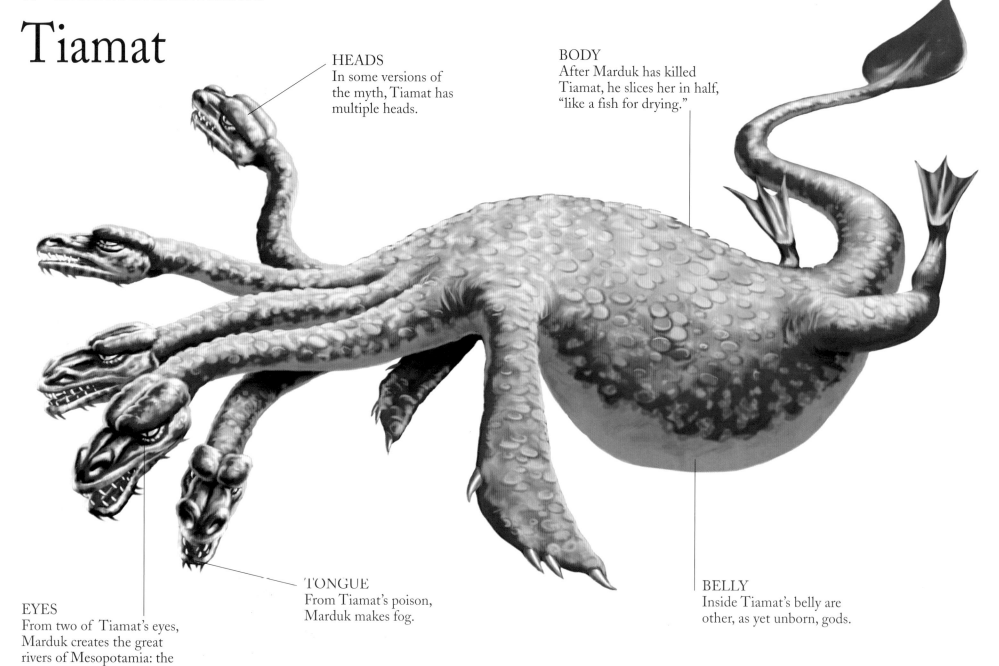

HEADS
In some versions of
the myth, Tiamat has
multiple heads.

BODY
After Marduk has killed
Tiamat, he slices her in half,
"like a fish for drying."

EYES
From two of Tiamat's eyes,
Marduk creates the great
rivers of Mesopotamia: the
Tigris and the Euphrates.

TONGUE
From Tiamat's poison,
Marduk makes fog.

BELLY
Inside Tiamat's belly are
other, as yet unborn, gods.

The story of Tiamat is one of the oldest stories in the world. According to the mythology of Mesopotamia, Tiamat is the dragon goddess of the sea. With Apsu, god of freshwaters, she has four children, who are also gods. These gods grow noisy, and Apsu wants to kill them. Ea, one of his children, discovers Apsu's plot and kills him first. Tiamat then plans to take revenge on her children and creates eleven fearsome monsters. Ea and others go into battle against Tiamat, but all fail. Then Ea's son, Marduk, offers to fight Tiamat if the other gods will make him their master after he defeats the dragon.

6 ft
(1.8 m)

SIZE COMPARISON

▶ MARDUK MAKES HIS WEAPONS, INCLUDING A NET, and gathers seven winds. He flies a storm chariot against Tiamat, spreads his net around her, and blows the winds at her with such force that they fill her body and she cannot close her mouth again. He fires an arrow that pierces her belly, splitting her in two. Her monsters try to flee, but he catches them. From one half of Tiamat, Marduk makes a roof for the sky; from the other half, he creates Earth. Now the gods consider Marduk the supreme god.

Where in the world?

The tablets telling the story of Marduk and Tiamat were discovered at the ruins of the city of Nineveh, which is near Mosul, Iraq, about 250 miles (400 km) northwest of Baghdad.

IRAQ

Did you know?

● Having defeated Tiamat, Marduk begins creating the world. He names the months of the year, makes the moon, and creates mankind to do the work of the gods so that the gods can rest and play.

● Marduk orders his city Babylon to be built. The ruins of this city are in Iraq, about 53 miles (85 km) south of Baghdad.

● Marduk's storm chariot is pulled by four beasts with venomous teeth.

● The story of Marduk and Tiamat probably dates from the eighteenth to the sixteenth century BCE. It was discovered in texts from 668 to 630 BCE.

● The earliest known map of the world, the Babylonian world map, made between about 700 and 500 BCE, includes the story of Tiamat and Marduk.

Typhon

EYES
Typhon's human-shaped head has fiery red eyes.

BODY
Typhon's body is covered in wings. He has scales all over his body.

VIPERS
Dozens of vipers coil from his neck and shoulders.

SIZE
Typhon is so big that he is taller than mountains, and his head often touches the stars.

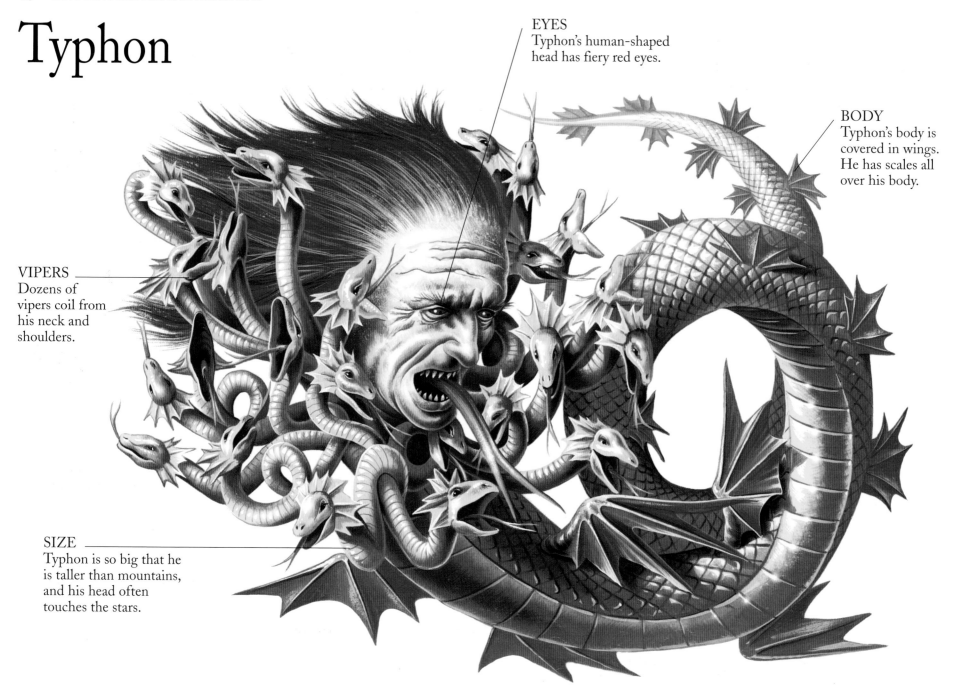

Typhon is known as the "father of all monsters" in Greek mythology. He is a giant (his upper body reaches as high as the stars), a dragon, and humanlike—all at the same time. He is related to the Titans, who are powerful gods. When Zeus, king of the Olympian gods, imprisons the Titans, Typhon sets out to avenge them. In his first battle with Zeus, Typhon tears out all of Zeus's sinews and leaves Zeus for dead in a cave. However, Hermes—Zeus's son and the messenger god—manages to return the sinews to Zeus. Restored to full health, he sets off after Typhon.

6 ft
(1.8 m)

SIZE COMPARISON

▶ TYPHON HAS BEEN DESTROYING CITIES. The Olympian gods, with the exception of Zeus, are so scared that they change themselves into animals. They flee to their home on Mount Olympus, leaving Zeus to battle Typhon alone. Mounted on a chariot drawn by winged horses, Zeus pursues Typhon across the heavens. Their battle causes earthquakes and tsunamis. Traveling across Greece, Typhon hurls whole mountains at Zeus. From Greece, Typhon flees to Sicily. Zeus finally traps Typhon by throwing one hundred lightning bolts at the dragon. Then, he finishes Typhon off by dropping Mount Etna on top of him.

Where in the world?

The fight rages across Greece down to Mount Etna on the island of Sicily, where, according to myths, Typhon still causes volcanic eruptions.

GREECE

SICILY

Did you know?

• In Greek mythology, Typhon is the father of hot, dangerous storm winds. Typhon's name might well be the origin of the word "typhoon."

• Typhon has many monstrous children, including Chimera, Cerberus, the Lernean Hydra, and the Ladon and Colchis dragons. His daughter Chimera looks like a lioness with a goat's head sticking out of the middle of her back and a snake for a tail. Cerberus is a three-headed dog who guards the entrance to the underworld. The Lernean Hydra is a nine-headed serpent. If someone cuts off one of her heads, two grow in its place.

• Typhon's wife Echidna, who is half woman, half serpent, is known as the "mother of all monsters."

Gong Gong

HEAD
When Gong Gong runs headfirst into Mount Buzhou, fire and water rush out, causing more devastation. The areas that escape the flood are destroyed by fire.

MOUTH
The Gong Gong eats all kinds of beasts using its powerful jaws and sharp teeth.

TOES
Gong Gong has twenty-one toes.

BODY
The Chinese dragon is made up of the horns of a deer, the neck of a snake, the scales of a carp, the claws of an eagle, and the ears of an ox.

Why do the rivers in China flow eastward toward the Pacific Ocean? Why is the Earth tilted on its axis? According to Chinese mythology, it is all because of a dragon. Gong Gong is the dragon god of water, but he is frustrated with his minor job of running errands in the court of heaven. He rebels against the emperor. With Xiang Yao, a nine-headed giant serpent, the dragon rampages across China, damming up rivers, creating floods, and polluting land. However, Gong Gong and Xiang Yao can defeat neither the powers of heaven nor Gong Gong's father, Zhu Rong. They must face this god of fire in battle.

6 ft
(1.8 m)

SIZE COMPARISON

▶ GONG GONG AND XIANG YAO BATTLE ZHU RONG ACROSS THE HEAVENS. Zhu Rong kills Xiang Yao, but the serpent's blood stinks so much that it pollutes the soil which it soaks into. Gong Gong realizes that he cannot defeat Zhu Rong and throws himself into Mount Buzhou, one of the eight pillars holding up the heavens. The mountain breaks in two, and the Earth shifts on its axis. And that is why all the rivers in China flow eastward and why the sun rises in the east and sets in the west.

Where in the world?

The mythical Mount Buzhou is in northwest China. Buzhou means "broken one" because Gong Gong breaks the mountain in two.

CHINA

Did you know?

● The dragon is the only mythological animal in the Chinese zodiac. The other animals are rat, ox, tiger, rabbit, snake, horse, goat, monkey, rooster, dog, and pig.

● Becoming a dragon in China is a blessing.

● One of Gong Gong's other assistants, Fuyou, flees to the bottom of the Huai River and turns into a red bear. Fuyou always smiles; however, anyone who meets him suffers misfortune.

● After Gong Gong has torn a hole in the sky, the goddess Nüwa manages to prop up the four points of the compass with the legs of a tortoise.

● There are 360 scaly creatures in Chinese mythology, and the dragon is considered the king of animals.

Bakunawa

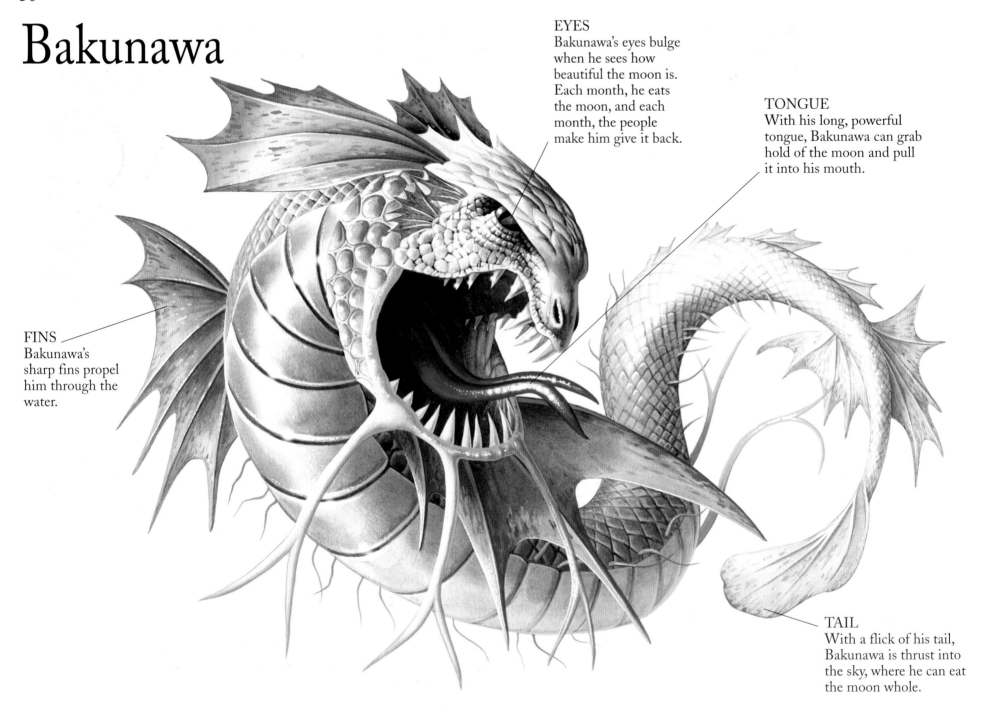

EYES
Bakunawa's eyes bulge when he sees how beautiful the moon is. Each month, he eats the moon, and each month, the people make him give it back.

TONGUE
With his long, powerful tongue, Bakunawa can grab hold of the moon and pull it into his mouth.

FINS
Bakunawa's sharp fins propel him through the water.

TAIL
With a flick of his tail, Bakunawa is thrust into the sky, where he can eat the moon whole.

According to Filipino mythology, the god Bathala created seven moons. To the sea dragon Bakunawa, these moons look so beautiful that he leaps from the water and gobbles them up. Without the moons, the Filipino people despair. They pray to Bathala, who tells them to go to sea in their boats, banging pots and pans. When they do this, Bakunawa is so disturbed that he spits out one of the moons, allowing it to rise again in the sky. However, the next month he cannot resist the temptation and eats the moon again, so once more the people take to their boats and make him give it back.

SIZE COMPARISON

▶ IN ONE PARTICULAR TALE ABOUT BAKUNAWA, the sea dragon falls in love with a girl. When the head of the girl's tribe finds out about the relationship, he burns the girl's house to the ground. Bakunawa is so angry that he eats all seven moons. As a punishment, Bathala banishes Bakunawa. The moons are returned and rise each month. But, people say, when there is a lunar eclipse and the moon does not appear at all, that is Bakunawa trying to come back.

Where in the world?

Bakunawa comes from the Philippines in Southeast Asia. There are more than 7,100 islands in the Philippines.

PHILIPPINES

Did you know?

• While the story of Bakunawa is about the moon, there is a similar story about the tides. Bakunawa has a sister who is a sea turtle. Whenever she visits another island to lay eggs, she seems to drag the sea with her like a tide. Fearing that she will drag so much sea with her that the island will disappear underwater, the local people kill her.

• Bakunawa appears in Filipino children's games and nursery rhymes.

• Haliya, goddess of the moon and of women, is the enemy of Bakunawa. A ritual dance is performed in honor of Haliya to ward off Bakunawa.

• On one globe from about 1510, a mapmaker wrote over Southeast Asia: "Here Are Dragons." It is possible the mapmaker meant Komodo dragons or was just referring to an unexplored region of the world. On ancient Roman and medieval maps, mapmakers would write over unexplored areas, "Here Are Lions."

Rong

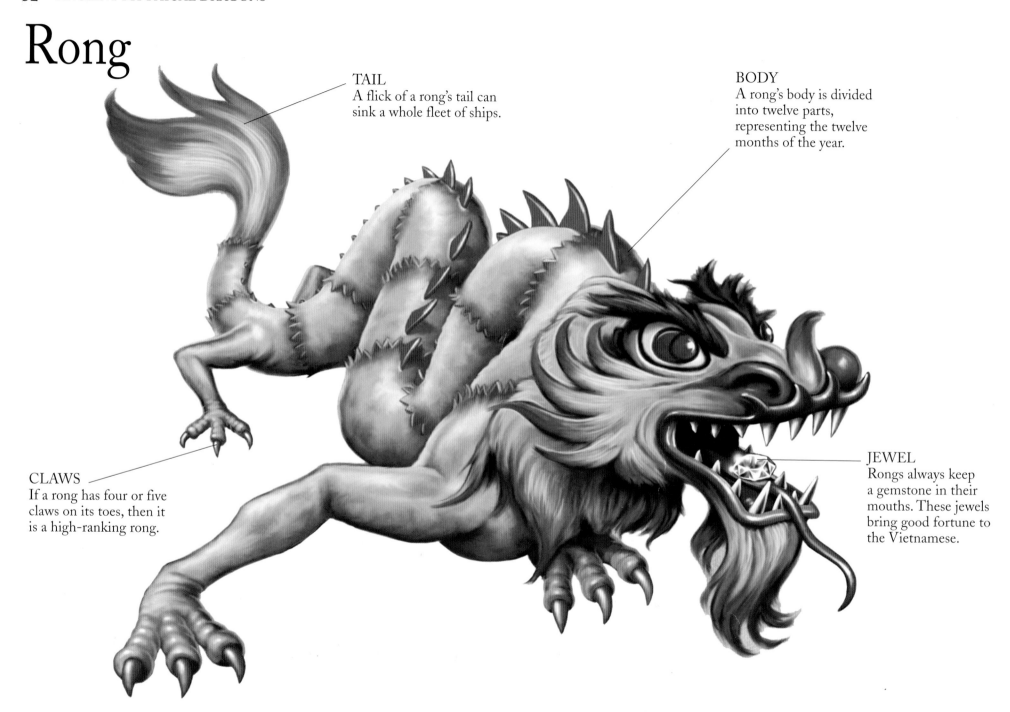

TAIL
A flick of a rong's tail can sink a whole fleet of ships.

BODY
A rong's body is divided into twelve parts, representing the twelve months of the year.

CLAWS
If a rong has four or five claws on its toes, then it is a high-ranking rong.

JEWEL
Rongs always keep a gemstone in their mouths. These jewels bring good fortune to the Vietnamese.

A rong is a cross between a crocodile, a snake, a lizard, and a bird. In Vietnamese folklore, people often have their origins in dragons and fairies. One of the founders of the Viet people was Lac Long Quan, who was descended from a dragon, while his wife, Au Co, was descended from a fairy. It was said that the dragons lived near the coast, while the fairies lived in the mountains. Rongs can change the weather and guard crops. Strongly influenced by Chinese culture, the image of the rong has changed over the centuries. Some have cat heads, other heads look more like a lion, and some have horns.

6 ft
(1.8 m)

SIZE COMPARISON

▶ WHEN NORTHERN INVADERS APPROACH VIETNAM IN THEIR SHIPS, the Vietnamese are overwhelmed and retreat farther and farther. Then, the rong dragons appear from the depths. They spit the gems they keep in their mouths into the water in front of the advancing ships. Immediately, steep, rocky islands spring up in the path of the invaders. It is too late for the invaders to change course, and their ships crash onto the rocks. The attack is defeated, Vietnam is saved, and the two thousand steep, rocky islands can be seen today in Ha Long Bay.

Where in the world?

Ha Long Bay lies off eastern Vietnam in the South China Sea. Ha Long means "descending dragon" in Vietnamese because, according to another story, the position of the islands shows where a dragon landed in the sea.

VIETNAM

Did you know?

● Where Vietnam's Mekong River reaches the sea, it divides into nine rivers, forming a delta. This region is called the Cuu Long, which means "nine dragons."

● At Vietnamese New Year, children dance a dragon dance to ward off evil spirits and bring good luck.

● Called a Giao Long, the first kind of Vietnamese dragon was a cross between a crocodile and a snake.

● The Vietnamese have stopped Chinese invaders three times in Ha Long Bay. In 1288, they stopped Mongol ships and managed to sink the fleet.

Illuyanka

(eel-oo-YANK-ha)

SERPENT
In the first version of the story, Illuyanka is a sea serpent, but in the second version he is a land monster.

HEAD
Some versions of the story say that Illuyanka has many heads, others that the dragon has just one.

BODY
Illuyanka is so big that he can wrap his body around all the gods in the world.

In Hittite mythology, the storm god Tarhunt battles the serpent dragon Illuyanka. The dragon defeats Tarhunt, who goes to the goddess Inara for help. In the countryside she finds a mortal, Hupasyia, who has a wife and children, but is so overwhelmed by the goddess's beauty that he leaves his family and goes with Inara. She prepares a huge feast for Illuyanka. When Illuyanka falls over drunk, Hupasyia ties up the dragon and Tarhunt cuts off the dragon's head.

6 ft
(1.8 m)

SIZE COMPARISON

Although Inara warns him not to look, once Hupasyia sees his wife and children in the fields again, he asks Inara to allow him to return home. The tale was recited at New Year's festivals.

► IN ANOTHER VERSION OF THE STORY, Illuyanka takes Tarhunt's eyes and heart. Wanting his revenge, Tarhunt marries a mortal and has a son, Sarruma. When Sarruma grows up, he marries Illuyanka's daughter. Tarhunt asks Illuyanka to return Tarhunt's eyes and heart as a wedding gift. But once Illuyanka has given back the eyes and heart, Tarhunt regains his old strength. He sets off for the coast and fights Illuyanka once again. This time he defeats Illuyanka. Sarruma is so upset that his father has killed Illuyanka that he asks Tarhunt to kill him, too. So, Tarhunt murders his son.

Where in the world?

TURKEY

The story of Illuyanka is known from stone tablets found in Çorum-Bojazköy, the site of the former Hittite capital, in present-day Turkey.

Did you know?

● The story was written down on clay tablets between 1050 and 850 BCE, but the story itself is from the period of about 1750 to 1500 BCE. It was written in cuneiform, which is a system of writing based on pictures rather than on an alphabet. Cuneiform languages were used for more than two thousand years, but their use died out in the second century CE. All understanding of cuneiform script was lost until the system was studied and translated in the nineteenth century.

● We do not know if Hupasyia succeeded in returning to his wife or not because some of the final tablets of the story are missing.

● The Hittite people lived in the region of modern-day Turkey and Syria. The Hittite Empire lasted from around the eighteenth century BCE to the twelfth century BCE.

● Sarruma is often shown riding a tiger and carrying an axe.

The Colchis Dragon

(KOL-kis)

BODY
The Colchis dragon has a long, snaky body.

EYES
The Colchis dragon's eyes never blink and it never falls asleep.

HISS
When the Colchis dragon hisses, the sound can be heard for miles around; babies wake up from their sleep and start crying.

TEETH
In one version of the story, Jason is first devoured by and then spat out by the Colchis dragon before he manages to steal the Golden Fleece.

In ancient Greek mythology, the Colchis dragon guards the Golden Fleece—the hair made of gold that was once the coat of a winged, flying ram. The son of a Greek king, Jason must steal the Golden Fleece to gain his rightful throne. His uncle Pelias had taken Jason's father's throne and will give it to Jason only if he steals the fleece for him. For this mission, Jason assembles a group of heroes who sail in a ship named the *Argo*. They are known as the Argonauts and have many adventures before reaching the kingdom of Colchis and the Colchis dragon.

6 ft
(1.8 m)

SIZE COMPARISON

▶ WHEN JASON REACHES THE KINGDOM OF COLCHIS, King Aeetes promises to give him the fleece if he can complete three additional tasks. Medea, the daughter of Aeetes, falls in love with Jason and helps him with each task. She gives him a magic ointment to rub over his body and his shield to protect him against attack by fire or iron. She also makes a potion that Jason uses to send the dragon to sleep. Jason is then able to creep behind the dragon, steal the fleece that is hanging from an oak tree, and escape from Colchis with Medea.

Where in the world?

● THESSALY

GEORGIA ●

Colchis is on the Black Sea coast of Georgia in the Caucasus region. Jason is from Iolcos in Thessaly on the mainland of Greece.

Did you know?

● The Colchis dragon is the son of the dragon Typhon.

● Argo means "swift" in Greek. Among the Argonauts are the heroes Orpheus and Heracles.

● Jason's adventures include defeating Talos, the giant man made of bronze, and navigating through the clashing rocks of Symplegades.

● The other two tasks King Aeetes sets for Jason are to plow a field with fire-breathing oxen and to sow a field with the teeth of another dragon. The teeth immediately grow into warriors, who attack Jason. Following Medea's advice, however, Jason throws a rock among them. They turn on each other, trying to find out which one of them threw the stone.

Apalala

LOWER BODY
By flexing his muscular, serpentine lower body back and forth, the dragon propels himself through the air and water.

TAIL
A dorsal fin along the dragon's tail acts as a rudder that steers the creature through both waters and skies.

FEET
Birdlike feet possess claws that shred the clouds to tatters and release the flooding rains.

HEAD
Apalala's human head forever bears the enraged and anguished expression of a soul betrayed. His shrieks send farmers scurrying home for cover.

UPPER BODY
The upper half of Apalala's body is human. Although he lacks wings, he is one of the best fliers among dragons.

Apalala is a powerful naga, a water dragon who controls the rains and rivers. A wise and cunning dragon, Apalala prevents evil dragons from creating violent rainstorms and floods. The people of his land are grateful for his protection. Their crops are healthy and abundant. Each year they present Apalala with a tribute of grain to thank him. However, after many years without damaging floods, some of the people stop giving Apalala their yearly tribute of grain. This neglect angers Apalala and he changes into a dangerous dragon. He terrifies the people and destroys all the crops with heavy rains and floods.

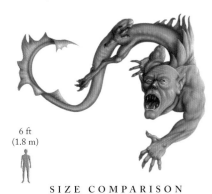

6 ft
(1.8 m)

SIZE COMPARISON

▶ ONE DAY THE BUDDHA comes to Apalala's land and feels compassion for the people whose crops are being destroyed by the angry dragon. The Buddha speaks with Apalala and convinces him that plaguing the countryside with floods is wrong. Apalala converts to Buddhism and promises not to rage against the countryside any longer. He merely asks that he be given one crop every twelve years. So every twelve years there are heavy rains in the land and Apalala receives the flooded crop as a gift.

Where in the world?

Apalala, the powerful water-dwelling dragon who controls rains and floods, makes his home in the Swat River of Pakistan.

● PAKISTAN

Did you know?

● After his conversion to Buddhism, Apalala created only enough yearly rainfall to ensure the crops would be healthy. The prosperity of all the farmers depends upon the goodwill of Apalala.

● In Kashmir, springs are the main source of water. Numerous temples dedicated to the worship of nagas were built near springs.

● In Buddhism, an animal is not allowed to become a monk. There was once a naga who wanted to be a monk so badly that he changed into human form. When he fell asleep, he changed back into a naga. Buddha told him he could not become a monk and the naga wept bitterly. Out of compassion for the naga, Buddha declared that all candidates for monkhood be called "Naga."

Neak

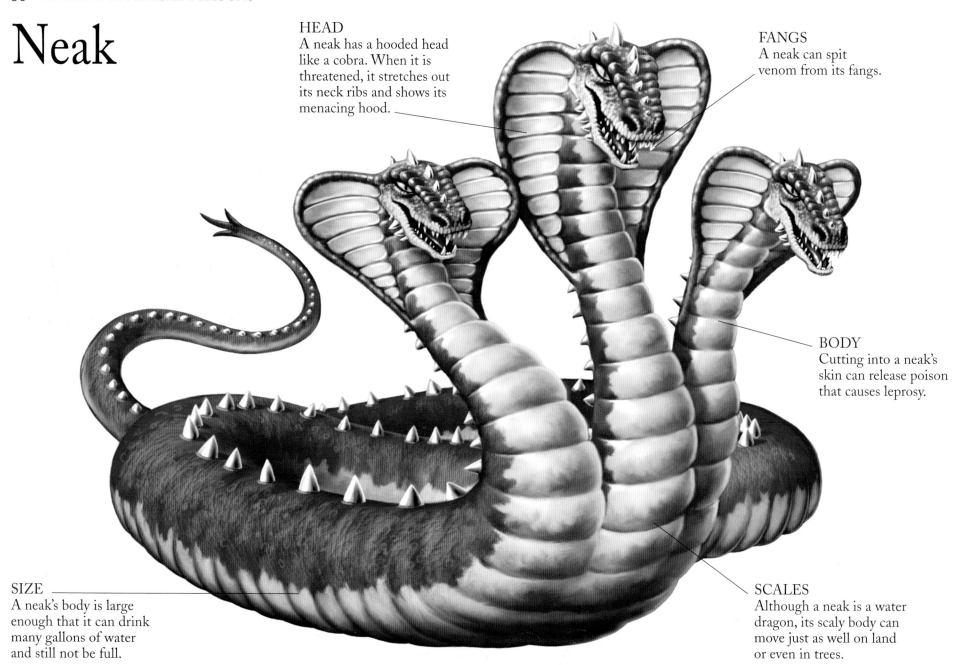

HEAD
A neak has a hooded head like a cobra. When it is threatened, it stretches out its neck ribs and shows its menacing hood.

FANGS
A neak can spit venom from its fangs.

BODY
Cutting into a neak's skin can release poison that causes leprosy.

SIZE
A neak's body is large enough that it can drink many gallons of water and still not be full.

SCALES
Although a neak is a water dragon, its scaly body can move just as well on land or even in trees.

Neaks are water dragons, related to nagas from Indian Hindu mythology. If a neak has an even number of heads, it is female and represents life and the earth. If it has an odd number of heads, it is male and represents spirituality and immortality. The more heads a neak has, the higher its rank. The highest number of heads is usually nine. Seven-headed neaks represent the seven colors of the rainbow. In Cambodian mythology, an Indian called Kaundinya invades Cambodia. Neang Neak, a Cambodian dragon princess, defends her country against him. When she is defeated, however, she happily marries Kaundinya. All the Khmer people are said to be descended from their marriage.

6 ft
(1.8 m)

SIZE COMPARISON

▶ ONE DAY, A KING OF CAMBODIA SUMMONS ALL HIS MINISTERS to a meeting at his palace in Angkor. One of his ministers is a neak and appears as a dragon rather than transforming himself into a human. The neak refuses to show respect to the king. Filled with anger, the king takes his sacred sword and attacks the neak, killing the dragon. Venomous spit sprays onto the king, scorching his skin and infecting him with leprosy. After that he is known as the leper king.

Where in the world?

The Neak comes from Cambodia in Southeast Asia. It is believed that Kaundinya landed at Tonle Sap, the largest freshwater lake in Southeast Asia.

● CAMBODIA

Did you know?

● The marriage of Kaundinya and Neang Neak represents the mix of Indian and Cambodian people and culture in Cambodia.

● From the thirteenth century onward, the Cambodians believed that the city of Angkor had once been ruled by a leper king. However, there is uncertainty as to which king this was.

● According to the myth, Neang Neak's dragon father is so happy with her marriage that he drinks up all the surplus water in Cambodia, reducing the water level so that the land is good for farming and building.

● Among the ruins of the old city at Angkor is an ornamental lake called Neak Pean, the island of serpents. Angkor was the seat of the Khmer Empire from the ninth to the fifteenth century CE, when it was the most powerful empire in Southeast Asia.

Futs-Lung

BODY
Futs-Lung can transform himself into any shape he desires or make himself completely invisible. He creates new hills when he hunches his back underground.

FIN
The scalloped dorsal fin along the length of his back stabilizes the dragon as he moves at lightning-fast speeds.

EYES
The dragon's bulging eyes can see into the depths of the earth where his treasure is stored.

CHIN
Hidden beneath his chin is the pearl of wisdom. The pearl glows from within and is a vessel of health.

JAWS
Futs-Lung's voice is like the jingling of copper pans, banging gongs, or ringing bells, depending upon his mood. His furious roar causes earthquakes.

The dragon of hidden treasures that lives deep within the earth is Futs-Lung. He guards all the precious gems and priceless metals in his lair. Futs-Lung possesses a magic pearl that multiplies when touched. Since the pearl represents wisdom, it is considered the most valuable of all the dragon's treasures. It takes 3,000 years for Futs-Lung to grow to his terrific adult size. Newly hatched, he looks much like an eel. By 500 years of age, Futs-Lung has grown a head that resembles a carp's. By his 1,500th birthday, he will grow a long tail, a head with a thick beard, and four stumpy legs with claws. At the age of 2,000, Futs-Lung will have horns.

6 ft
(1.8 m)

SIZE COMPARISON

▶ IN MODERN-DAY HONG KONG there is an apartment complex that was built near a mountain where Futs-Lung lives. The complex was designed with a large gap in the middle so that Futs-Lung's ocean view would remain unobstructed and his goodwill would be maintained. Like most Chinese dragons, Futs-Lung is benevolent until offended. His wrath should not be roused. He must be treated with respect and reverence so he does not unleash his incredible temper. Volcanoes are formed when Futs-Lung bursts from the earth and reports to heaven.

Where in the world?

Futs-Lung is the underworld dragon of China. He is in charge of guarding all the precious metals and gems buried in the earth.

● CHINA

Did you know?

● Imperial Chinese dragons have five toes, Korean dragons four, and Japanese dragons three.

● Chinese dragons lay one egg at a time. Each dragon egg takes one thousand years to hatch.

● The Chinese refer to themselves as "descendants of the dragon."

● Chinese dragons have 117 scales on their serpentine bodies.

● It was a compliment to refer to someone as "dragon face" in China. Many founding emperors of dynasties were described as having dragon faces. It was considered a lucky sign indicating their future greatness.

● Chinese dragons are shape-shifters that can change into the form of a man, shrink themselves down to a mouse, or expand until they fill up the space between heaven and Earth.

Hatuibwari

(HAT-oo-ee-BWAH-ree)

HEAD
Four eyes indicate
Hatuibwari is wise
and all-seeing.

WINGS
Hatuibwari's wings
carry him back
and forth between
the sky and the
mountaintops
where he lives.
Since he has no
legs, strong wings
are necessary to
allow him to hover.

HANDS
The great, clawed hands carefully
shaped the first man and woman
in Melanesia from clay.

BODY
The serpentine shape of Hatuibwari's
torso cuts down on wind resistance and
is perfect for darting through the sky. It
is also a good shape for swimming fast
through water.

On San Cristóbal Island in Melanesia, the ancient belief is that the dragon Hatuibwari created and nourished all living things. He is the male version of Mother Earth, with a body that is half-human and half-snake. Two enormous wings carry him through the skies and four eyes allow him to see everything under the sun. Hatuibwari rolls red clay in his hands, breathes on it, and forms the shape of a human. He places the clay figure in the sun and it comes to life as the first woman. Later, while the first woman is asleep, Hatuibwari takes a rib from her side, adds more clay, and creates the first man.

6 ft
(1.8 m)

SIZE COMPARISON

▶ ONE DAY HATUIBWARI COILS AROUND HIS HUMAN GRANDSON to comfort him. The child's father comes home and mistakes Hatuibwari for an enormous serpent squeezing the life from his child. The frightened father does not recognize the dragon spirit as his father-in-law and cuts Hatuibwari to pieces with a knife. The pieces unite again at once. Angry and offended, Hatuibwari announces that he is leaving and will cause the people's crops to fail. Hatuibwari departs to live on Guadalcanal Island and everything deteriorates in his absence.

Where in the world?

Hatuibwari lives in the sky and on sacred mountaintops of San Cristóbal and Guadalcanal in the Solomon Islands, Melanesia.

SOLOMON ●
ISLANDS

AUSTRALIA

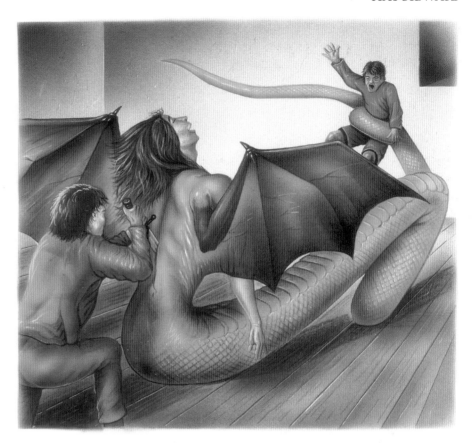

Did you know?

● Hatuibwari often appears in a sacred grove. Anyone who does not treat the grove with proper reverence and respect is stricken with illness and terrible sores.

● Sacrifices of pigs are offered to Hatuibwari to appease him. Like Chinese and Japanese dragons, he must be treated with respect or he will grow angry.

● Hatuibwari causes rains to fall in order to quench his thirst.

● Babylonian, Chinese, Australian, and Aztec mythologies all contain stories of dragons as creators of life on Earth.

● In Melanesian mythology, Darkness, Forever, and the Sea have always existed. Hatuibwari created animals, food, trees, and humans. He travels between our world and the sky.

Jawzahr

TAIL
A spade-shaped tuft at the end of his tail indicates Jawzahr is a male. Female dragons lack this tuft.

HEAD
Jawzahr's huge, horned head is able to live independently from his body. His eyes glint with perpetual malice.

JAWS
Gaping jaws capable of devouring the sun or moon in one gulp produce a furious screech that can be heard across a continent.

CLAWS
Used for grasping tree branches or stone outcroppings back when he lived on Earth, Jawzahr's claws now grip at the air in a blind rage as he flies through the night skies.

WINGS
Jawzahr's wings are made of strong but lightweight bone. Thin, leathery skin is stretched across the framework of bone, making Jawzahr the best flier of any dragon.

In ancient Persia, eclipses occur when Jawzahr the comet dragon swallows the sun or moon. He menaces the two, chasing them around the sky and eating them at regular intervals. Jawzahr commands a legion of demons and is a crafty, curious dragon. He disguises himself as a god one day and drinks an immortality-giving potion meant only for the gods. The sun and moon, however, see everything and they report Jawzahr's trickery to the gods. As punishment, Jawzahr's head is severed with one well-aimed throw of a discus. But Jawzahr is already immortal because of the potion he drank, and he cannot be killed.

SIZE COMPARISON

▶ ENRAGED, JAWZAHR ASCENDS TO THE SKY. The two immortal parts of him live on, separate from each other. Jawzahr is angry at both the sun and moon for revealing his deception to the gods. He forever chases the sun and moon, gobbling them down when he catches them. Anytime an eclipse occurs, it means that Jawzahr has caught up with and consumed the sun or the moon. As for his tail, it emits a shower of comets that stream across the night sky.

Where in the world?

A dragon from Islamic mythology, Jawzahr first made his appearance in legends from Persia, which is modern-day Iran.

● IRAN

Did you know?

● The astronomical location of the dragon's head and dragon's tail mark the points where solar and lunar eclipses may occur.

● Draco, a constellation in the northern hemisphere, gets its name from the Latin word for dragon. One of the brightest stars in Draco is in its tail and is named Thuban, which is the Arabic word for dragon. Another star in Draco is Rastaban, which means "head of the dragon." About 5,000 years ago Thuban was the Pole Star, Earth's North Star. The ancient Egyptians recognized Thuban as the North Star at the time they were constructing the Great Pyramid. Today our North Star is Polaris.

● Many ancient cultures believed that comets were dragons streaking across the sky.

Ladon

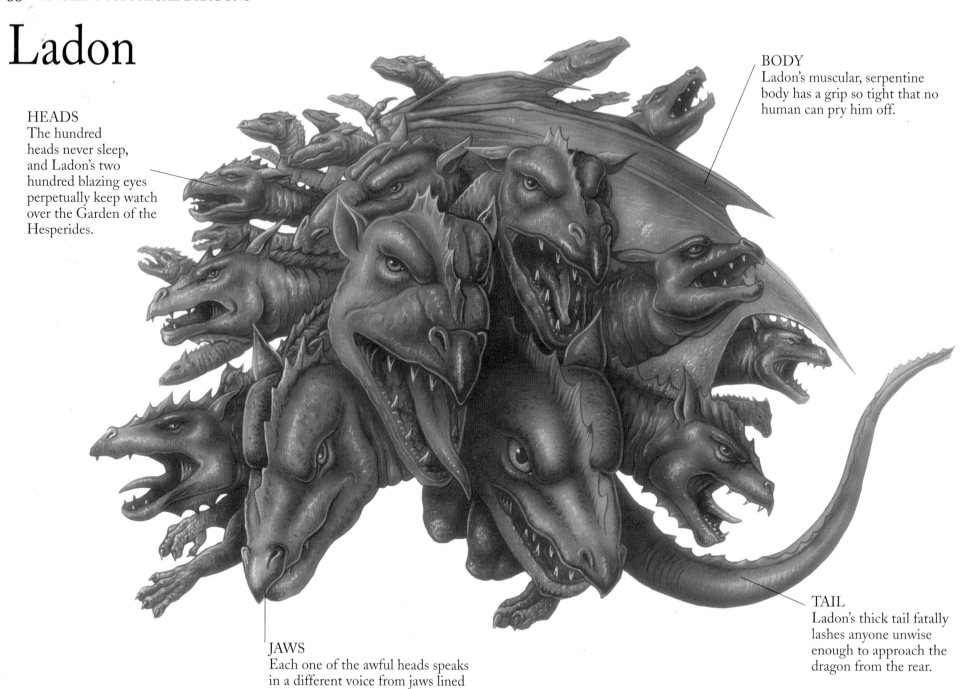

HEADS
The hundred heads never sleep, and Ladon's two hundred blazing eyes perpetually keep watch over the Garden of the Hesperides.

BODY
Ladon's muscular, serpentine body has a grip so tight that no human can pry him off.

JAWS
Each one of the awful heads speaks in a different voice from jaws lined with teeth as sharp as knives.

TAIL
Ladon's thick tail fatally lashes anyone unwise enough to approach the dragon from the rear.

In Greek mythology there is a monstrous dragon with a hundred heads who twines his serpentine body around a tree bearing golden apples. This beast is Ladon, and he was placed in the Garden of the Hesperides by Hera, queen of the Olympians. His task is to guard the garden and its golden apples. Not one of Ladon's hundred heads ever sleeps and each head speaks with a different voice. Ladon's two hundred fiery, watchful eyes ensure that no one approaches the golden apples. Anyone who dares to sail to the ends of the earth in search of Hera's golden apples risks being torn to pieces by Ladon's gigantic teeth or squeezed to death in the coils of his muscular body.

6 ft
(1.8 m)

SIZE COMPARISON

▶ THE KING OF MYCENAE TESTS HERACLES by assigning him twelve labors. The eleventh labor requires Heracles to steal the golden apples that Ladon guards. Heracles dips his arrow tips in the gall of a hydra and fires the poisoned arrows over the garden wall at Ladon. The awful dragon is felled by the poisoned arrows and Heracles enters the garden safely. He steals the apples and completes his eleventh labor. Passing sailors later report having seen the slain Ladon with only the tip of his tail still twitching.

Where in the world?

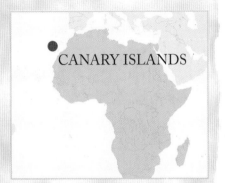

CANARY ISLANDS

The Garden of the Hesperides, where Ladon winds around the tree of golden apples, lies in the Canary Islands off the coast of Africa.

Did you know?

• Where blood from Ladon's wounds drenched the ground, dragon trees sprouted from each drop. Dragon trees have massive trunks and twisted branches. Their sap, called "dragon tree blood," is dark red and is believed to have healing properties.

• In Roman mythology, Heracles is known as Hercules and Hera is called Juno.

• The Latin word for a dragon, "draco," means snake or serpent.

• Direct frontal attack is the least effective way to slay a dragon. Heracles is wise enough to maintain a safe distance from the beast and use the stout garden wall as a shield.

Ryujin 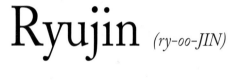 *(ry-oo-JIN)*

TAIL
A single thrash of Ryujin's tail creates massive tidal waves that wipe out entire coastal villages.

HEAD
The Ryujin's head has the horns of a stag, whiskers that indicate his wisdom, and eyes that see everything from the bottom of the ocean.

CLAWS
Floods happen when Ryujin rakes his impressive claws through the ocean. A swipe of his foot is capable of capsizing an entire fleet of ships.

BODY
Ryujin coils his massive, scaly body through the chambers of his underwater palace.

JAWS
When Ryujin opens his enormous, toothy jaws and inhales, giant whirlpools appear in the water.

In Japanese mythology, Ryujin is the dragon god of the sea. He lives beneath the ocean in a jeweled palace made of red and white coral. His palace has a snowy winter hall, a spring hall where cherry trees grow, a summer hall with chirping crickets, and a fall hall with colorful maple trees. For a human, one day at Ryujin's underwater palace is equal to a hundred years on Earth. Sea turtles, fish, and jellyfish act as the dragon god's loyal servants. Ryujin controls the tides with magical sea jewels. Humans must approach Ryujin carefully because no mortal can glimpse his entire body and survive the sight. When angry, Ryujin churns the waves, causing rough waters for sailors.

6 ft
(1.8 m)

SIZE COMPARISON

▶ THE EMPRESS JINGO asks Ryujin for assistance in the attack she plans against Korea. Ryujin's messenger brings her the two tide jewels. Jingo sails toward Korea with the Japanese fleet. The Korean fleet meets them at sea. Jingo flings the low-tide jewel into the sea and all the waters disappear, stranding the Korean ships. When the Korean soldiers leap from their ships to attack on foot, Jingo casts the high-tide jewel onto the seabed. All the waters rush back, drowning the Korean soldiers.

Where in the world?

Ryujin, the dragon god of the sea, lives at the bottom of the ocean near the Ryukyu Islands off the southern coast of Japan.

JAPAN

● RYUKYU ISLANDS

Did you know?

● Ryujin's beautiful daughter married Prince Hoori. This makes Ryujin the ancestor of all the Japanese emperors.

● Because Japanese dragons are related to royalty, no one is allowed to harm them. Since they have nothing to fear from humans, Japanese dragons have become tame over the years. Legend has it that dragons may be seen blocking traffic in cities or sunning themselves on rocks off Japan's shores.

● Many dragons are shape-shifters. They can change into the form of a human.

● In both Japan and China, the dragon is one of the guardian animals of the four directions. The dragon guards the eastern compass point and is associated with the season of spring.

Shen-Lung

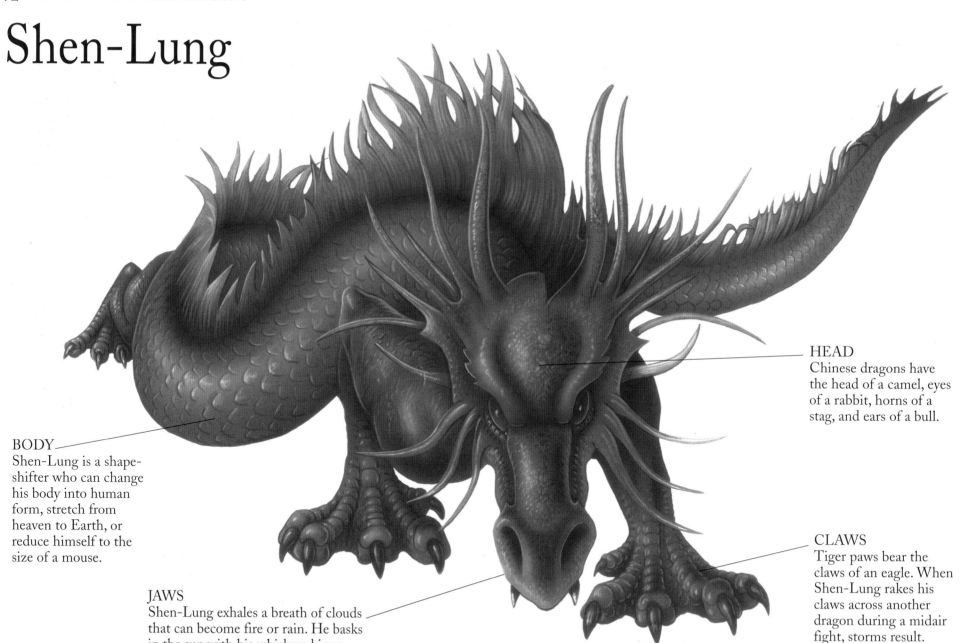

HEAD
Chinese dragons have the head of a camel, eyes of a rabbit, horns of a stag, and ears of a bull.

BODY
Shen-Lung is a shape-shifter who can change his body into human form, stretch from heaven to Earth, or reduce himself to the size of a mouse.

CLAWS
Tiger paws bear the claws of an eagle. When Shen-Lung rakes his claws across another dragon during a midair fight, storms result.

JAWS
Shen-Lung exhales a breath of clouds that can become fire or rain. He basks in the sun with his whiskered jaws hanging open, hoping that a delicious sparrow will land in his mouth.

In China, Shen-Lung is the spiritual dragon who is responsible for making weather. He controls rain, clouds, and wind, all of which are important in a country with so many farmers. The right amount of rain is essential for healthy crops, so his power over rain gives Shen-Lung the authority over life and death in China. Offerings to Shen-Lung assure a bountiful harvest. He must be approached with the utmost respect and reverence. It is important not to offend Shen-Lung because if he feels neglected his anger is aroused. The result of his wrath is terrible weather in the form of floods or drought, which could destroy the life-giving crops upon which the Chinese depend.

6 ft
(1.8 m)

SIZE COMPARISON

▶ BECAUSE OF HIS GREAT POWER, Shen-Lung grows lazy over the years. He shrinks himself to the size of a mouse in order to hide and avoid work. When lightning strikes a house or tree, it is because the thunder god is sending his servant to search for Shen-Lung. Shen-Lung floats across the sky, his body stretching farther than the eye can see. He is benevolent but bad-tempered. The worst floods in Chinese history were unleashed by Shen-Lung when he was offended by a mortal.

Where in the world?

Shen-Lung is the spiritual dragon who has control over the winds and the rains that affect all the crops grown in China.

● CHINA

Did you know?

● Shen-Lung's voice is heard in hurricanes and his claws can be seen in flashes of lightning.

● When Shen-Lung is sick, the rain has a distinctly fishy smell.

● The dragon is the emblem representing the Chinese emperor and the phoenix represents the empress. Together, the dragon and the phoenix are used as symbols of marital harmony.

● All Chinese dragons have nine distinct features: the head of a camel, scales of a carp, horns of a stag, eyes of a rabbit, ears of a bull, neck of a snake, belly of a clam, paws of a tiger, and the claws of an eagle.

● The ancient Chinese thought glass was solidified dragon breath.

Glaurung

TAIL
Glaurung's whiplike tail is a deadly weapon. A blow dealt by Glaurung's tail can crumble stone walls or snap a grown man's spine.

BODY
A glimmer of fire shows around the edges of his golden, armorlike scales when Glaurung is angry. His scales fade to a dull gray when his fury dies down.

EYES
Lidless, unblinking eyes cast a bewitching spell that makes his victims helpless. Everything Glaurung sees is telepathically transmitted to his evil master, Morgoth.

JAWS
Flames as hot as lava shoot from Glaurung's jaws, scorching everything within 40 feet (12 meters) of the beast. When not spouting fire, his breath has the putrid reek of decaying animal flesh.

Glaurung the Deceiver, or the Worm of Greed, is the Father of Dragons. Bred by Morgoth the Enemy, Glaurung uses trickery and deception to spread lies. He enjoys creating misery and confusion in others. The dragon wreaks as much havoc using the spells he casts as he does on the battlefield using brute force. Glaurung is corrupt and foul-smelling, able to taint pure waters with his mere presence. He serves as the eyes of evil Morgoth, who senses everything the dragon sees. Before he is fully mature, Glaurung participates in battle, but his armor is not fully hardened and cannot withstand the archers' arrows.

6 ft
(1.8 m)

SIZE COMPARISON

▶ GLAURUNG CASTS DRAGON SPELLS with his lidless, unblinking eyes. He fills the head of the heroic Túrin with lies and self-doubt. Túrin's sister, Nienor, is also a victim of Glaurung's spell. She is spellbound with complete forgetfulness and cannot remember her own name. As a result, Nienor unwittingly marries her brother. In order to slay the deceiver, Túrin clings to a cliffside above a deep gorge where Glaurung passes. When the dragon slithers overhead, Túrin kills Glaurung by thrusting his black sword into the beast's soft belly.

Where in the world?

Glaurung is the first and fiercest of the land-dwelling firedrakes of J.R.R. Tolkien's Middle Earth in *The Silmarillion*. Glaurung builds a nest upon the treasure in the tunnels beneath Nargothrond after the city is sacked.

● NARGOTHROND

Middle Earth

Did you know?

● When Glaurung dies, both Túrin and Nienor are released from the dragon's spell. Both commit suicide when they discover they have married a sibling.

● Blood issues from the fatal wound when Túrin pulls the black sword from Glaurung's body. The poisonous blood burns Túrin's hand.

● Glaurung, red-hot with wrath, lies in a river where he generates a horrible reek and foul vapors that blind people until they lose their way. Even horses are driven mad by the dragon's stench.

● Anyone foolish enough to look Glaurung directly in the eye is immediately rendered helpless by his dragon spell.

● Glaurung led the assault in the Battle of Sudden Flame, but was knifed in the belly and had to flee the battlefield to heal.

The Seven-Headed Dragon

HEADS
This dragon can talk.
When it meets the
huntsman it announces,
"Many knights have left
their lives here. I shall
soon have made an end
of thee, too."

TONGUES
After the huntsman
has killed the
dragon, he cuts out
its seven tongues.

FIRE
Using the breath from
its seven jaws, the
dragon sets the grass
on fire, hoping that the
smoke will choke the
huntsman.

In the Brothers Grimm tale "The Two Brothers," a huntsman defeats a dragon with the help of a hare, a fox, a wolf, a bear, and a lion. The huntsman and his animals arrive at a town terrorized by a dragon that is demanding the king's daughter as a sacrifice. Followed by his animals, the huntsman climbs the dragon's hill. In a church, he drinks three cups that promise to make him the strongest man on Earth. With his new strength, he is able to pull a special sword from the ground. As the dragon approaches, the huntsman locks the king's daughter in the church for safety. Now he has to face the dragon.

6 ft
(1.8 m)

SIZE COMPARISON

▶ THE DRAGON BREATHES FLAMES from its jaws and sets fire to the grass, hoping that the smoke will suffocate the huntsman. But the hare, the bear, the fox, the wolf, and the lion trample on the fire, putting it out. Then the dragon charges, but with his sword the huntsman strikes off three of the dragon's heads. When the dragon spits fire, the huntsman swings his sword again, cutting off three more dragon heads. As the dragon makes a final charge, the huntsman slices off its tail. The huntsman's animals then tear the dragon to pieces.

Did you know?

• The huntsman meets his five animals when he and his brother are looking for food. They are about to eat a hare when the hare begs for its life and promises them two young hares to eat instead. The brothers cannot find it in their hearts to kill the young hares, so they take them along. After that, the same situation happens with the other animals until there are ten animals altogether.

• Later in "The Two Brothers," the huntsman and his animals are in the forest and are turned to stone by a witch.

• "The Two Brothers" is a folktale collected by the Brothers Grimm, whose first collection of stories, *Children's and Household Tales*, was published in 1812.

• Among the most famous of the stories collected by the Brothers Grimm are "Snow White," "Hansel and Gretel," and "Little Red Riding Hood."

Where in the world?

The Brothers Grimm collected their stories from people across Germany, but some of the stories originated in other countries.

● GERMANY

The Red Dragon

WINGS
The red dragon has enormous wings that allow it to fight while airborne.

MOUTH
The sound of the red dragon's scream drains the color from men's faces and stops animals from being able to produce young.

COLORS
Merlin says that the red dragon is a symbol of the Celts, and the white dragon is a symbol of the invading Anglo-Saxon people.

In the story "Lludd and Lleuelys," a horrific scream tears through Great Britain. At the sound, children turn numb and plants shrivel up. King Lludd of Britain asks his brother, King Lleuelys of France, for help. Lleuelys explains that the sound is of the red and the white dragons fighting each other. He instructs Lludd to measure Britain to find the country's center. Lleuelys tells Lludd to then dig a hole at the

6 ft
(1.8 m)

SIZE COMPARISON

center and put an open container of mead (an alcoholic drink made from honey) in it. After that, he should cover the container with a silk cloth. But how is this going to free the British people from the fighting dragons?

▶ LLUDD HAS BRITAIN MEASURED, AND THE CENTER is found to be in the town of Oxford. The mead is put into the container in the ground, and the silk screen covers it. Lludd watches as the dragons fight, first in the sky, then on the ground. When they grow tired, they fall onto the silk screen and drag it down with them to the container of mead. They gulp down the mead and fall asleep. While they are asleep, Lludd wraps the silk around the dragons and encases them in a stone chest.

Where in the world?

The dragons are captured in Oxford, about 54 miles (87 km) from London, England. The dragons are said to be buried in Dinas Emrys, a rocky hill in northwestern Wales.

WALES

ENGLAND

Did you know?

• "Lludd and Lleuelys" is a Welsh tale written down in the twelfth or thirteenth century, but it is based on stories from the ninth century.

• Lleuelys also helps Lludd with two other problems: defeating a race of people who have taken over Britain and defeating a magician who has been stealing food from Lludd and his people.

• In a related tale, the tyrant Vortigern tries to build a castle at Dinas Emrys in Wales, but the castle keeps collapsing. Believing the site to be cursed, Vortigern prepares to sacrifice a boy to break the spell. However, the boy, Merlin (who grows up to be the famous wizard), explains that the castle collapses because the two dragons from "Lludd" and "Lleuelys" are buried beneath it. Vortigern later releases the dragons, and they fight, the red one defeating the white one.

• Today, Wales and Bhutan are the only two countries with dragons on their flags.

Hungarian Horntail

HEAD
The terrible head has bronze horns used to gore victims. The dragon's hearing is so good that it can detect any threat from a long distance.

TAIL
A whip of the spike-lined tail can easily deal a killing blow to the dragon's enemies.

EYES
The yellow eyes have a reflective layer that enables the dragon to detect things five times more effectively than a human can.

CLAWS
Its sharp, curved claws are used to slash at the flesh of enemies or grip its victim's body.

JAWS
When not making a yowling scream that curdles the blood, the dragon shoots a stream of fire that reaches as far as 50 feet (15 m).

As the first task of the Triwizard Tournament in J.K. Rowling's *Harry Potter and the Goblet of Fire*, Harry must get past a mother Hungarian Horntail and steal a golden egg from her nest. The golden egg is placed among her clutch of gray eggs. A nesting mother Horntail is especially hazardous when defending her young. Harry summons his racing broom and uses it to fly back and forth,

6 ft
(1.8 m)

SIZE COMPARISON

taunting the dragon. He dodges blasts of fire deftly on his broom, but has one shoulder scraped by the Horntail's thrashing, spiked tail. He lures the furious dragon up onto her hind legs by flying high above her, then swoops down and snatches the golden egg.

▶ THE HUNGARIAN HORNTAIL IS REMARKABLY DANGEROUS because it can do as much damage with its spike-lined tail as it can with its fanged mouth, which shoots jets of fire up to a distance of 50 feet (15 m). The young use their spiked tails to smash their way out of their eggs. It can require anywhere from six to eight well-trained wizards to subdue a fully grown Hungarian Horntail with stunning spells. It is considered the most dangerous of all dragon breeds, according to the Ministry of Magic.

Where in the world?

Normally native to Hungary, smuggling of the Hungarian Horntail's eggs has led to sightings of the dragon in England.

● HUNGARY

Did you know?

● The blood, heart, horn, hide, and liver of dragons all have magical properties.

● There are ten breeds of purebred dragon that can interbreed and produce hybrid dragons.

● The female dragon is larger and more aggressive than the male dragon.

● The motto for Hogwarts School of Witchcraft and Wizardry—*Draco Dormiens Nunquam Titillandus*—means "Never tickle a sleeping dragon."

● The dinosaur *Dracorex Hogwartsia*, which means "dragon king of Hogwarts," was named by young visitors to the Children's Museum of Indianapolis.

● The Ministry of Magic has classified the Hungarian Horntail as a known wizard-killer.

Tintaglia

(tin-TAG-lee-ah)

MIND
She thinks humans are inferior, but she still likes to be flattered by them.

WINGS
The skin on her wings is transparent in the sunlight.

EYES
When she is angry, her eyes swirl and change color.

TEETH
Her teeth, blood, scales, and claws are all wanted by humans for their healing properties.

THROAT
From the sac on Tintaglia's throat, she sprays her victims with acid.

TALONS
She uses her talons to clutch her prey, whether it is a human or a deer, to eat.

What if there were only one dragon left on Earth? That is what happens in Robin Hobb's *Realm of the Elderlings* novels. Dragons have been wiped out except for Tintaglia, who was protected in her cocoon. Now she is trying to find out if there are any other dragons alive. However, it is believed that parts of a dragon's body can heal humans, so people are trying to kill her. She has the power to turn people into "Elderlings," who are humans that once lived in such harmony with dragons that they developed dragonlike features. Their bodies stretched out, they grew scales and clawed fingernails, and they lived for up to four hundred years.

6 ft
(1.8 m)

SIZE COMPARISON

▶ A MOTHER, KEFFRIA, SCREAMS AT TINTAGLIA, telling her that the dragon might as well kill her because Tintaglia has already taken her daughter to turn her into an Elderling. A drop of spit falls from Tintaglia's mouth and burns its way through the ground. A crowd of people gathers together to resist Tintaglia. She may have charmed them before but they realize now that she is only using them. Her silver eyes swivel, and she fixes a man with such an intense stare that he can hear her thoughts telling him what a little fool he is.

Where in the world?

Rain Wilds

FRENGONG

Before Tintaglia hatched as a dragon, she was enclosed in a cocoon in the ruins of the Elderling city of Frengong, in an area known as the Rain Wilds.

Did you know?

• Like all dragons in the *Elderling* books, Tintaglia is arrogant and vain. She regards humans as inferior creatures, whose only purpose is to serve her.

• These dragons have long lives and refer to humans as "creatures of a few breaths" because their lives are so short in comparison.

• These dragons are born like turtles are; the queen dragon lays eggs on a special beach. Later, serpents emerge from these eggs and make their way to the sea. They live in the sea for several years until they are fully grown, which means they are big enough to overturn a boat. They return to the same beach and build a cocoon. When they come out of the cocoon, they are no longer serpents but fully formed dragons.

The Northern Dragon

EYES
Even after John has first stabbed the dragon, he looks at John with cold, cruel eyes. There is not a spark of rage in them.

MOUTH
When the dragon is wounded, he opens his mouth wide. The inside is gray, like lead, and his breath is freezing cold.

HEAD
When the dragon first appears out of the cave, he bobs his head like a caterpillar; the front half of his body moves while the back half is steady.

TAIL
The dragon's long tail can be used to loop around enemies and hold them.

Why do dragons usually live alone? In the case of the Northern Dragon, it is because he enjoys eating other dragons too much. The Northern Dragon has eaten all the other dragons, including his own dragon wife! "Often I wish I hadn't eaten my wife," he says, but he admits that he would not be a dragon if he had not eaten her. He guards his hoard of gold in his mountain cave. He tries to stay alert all the time because he imagines that people are plotting to steal his gold. He thinks they are cruel for not allowing him any rest. In fact, no one is at all interested in his gold.

6 ft
(1.8 m)

SIZE COMPARISON

▶ YOUNG JOHN HAS BEEN SENT TO SLAY THE NORTHERN DRAGON. In the mists, he sees the dragon stretching out of its cave above him. The dragon loops right around John and back into the cave. He begins to tighten his body around John's chest. John ducks down and jabs his sword into the underside of the dragon. The dragon's head twists back out of the cave. As soon as the dragon's cold breath touches John's face, John changes. He will never again feel panic or greed, and his strength multiplies. This time he stabs the dragon, killing it.

Where in the world?

The Northern Dragon lives on a barren, rocky mountain, but the story takes place in a fictitious landscape.

Did you know?

● The Northern Dragon appears in C. S. Lewis's novel *The Pilgrim's Regress*, published in 1933. C. S. Lewis is best known as the author of *The Chronicles of Narnia* novels. He taught at the University of Oxford in Great Britain. There, he was friends with J. R. R. Tolkien, who is the author of *The Hobbit*, *The Lord of the Rings*, and *Farmer Giles of Ham*.

● In *The Pilgrim's Regress*, young John goes on a spiritual journey across many lands and has many adventures. He has to fight the Northern Dragon because John is too swayed by his feelings. Killing the Northern Dragon gives John the strength of body and mind that the dragon possessed. Now, John has a balance of feelings and strength.

● The dragon saying in Latin is: *serpens nisi serpentem comederit*, which, translated loosely, means: "worm grows not to dragon till he eats worm."

Luckdragon

BACK
Falkor's enormous back can carry heroes through the air on important quests.

EYES
The luckdragon is able to spot landmarks far below him on the ground even when traveling through the clouds at top speed.

JAWS
Falkor's lionlike mouth produces a blue flame. The luckdragon is the only dragon known to spew blue fire.

BODY
The long, graceful body with pearl-colored scales requires no wings for flying. The luckdragon uses levitation for flight rather than normal dragon wings.

A dragon species in Michael Ende's novel *The Neverending Story*, the luckdragon is a wingless beast that flies by levitating. Falkor, the luckdragon in the novel, is unlike the traditional terrifying dragon. He is an optimist, believing in the power of good luck and perseverance. He tells young Atreyu that if he never gives up, good luck will find him. Even when Falkor is trapped in an enormous web stretched across Deep Chasm and struggling against a swarm of poisonous insects, he does not give up. Falkor credits Atreyu with helping him escape the web. He carries the boy on his back in search of the Southern Oracle.

6 ft
(1.8 m)

SIZE COMPARISON

▶ FALKOR IS AS TALENTED AS HE IS KIND. Despite his enormous size, he is as light as a summer cloud and needs no wings to fly. He can fly while sleeping, fly on his back, and perform perfect loop-the-loops. Falkor whizzes through the mists and shreds of clouds so rapidly that Atreyu gasps for breath. When circling the night sky above the Lake of Tears, Falkor sings a song of pure joy in his bell-like voice, which is so beautiful it opens the heart of every listener.

Where in the world?

Falkor the luckdragon lives in the land of Fantastica, a place where the geography is ever-changing because it is determined by wishes.

Fantastica

LAKE OF TEARS

Did you know?

● Luckdragons feed on air and heat. They require no other food. Without air and heat they live only a short time.

● Viewed from Earth, a luckdragon flying overhead resembles a slow flash of lightning or a white flame.

● The rider traveling on the back of a luckdragon experiences a smooth ride despite the great speed of travel.

● As a creature of air and fire, the luckdragon fears and hates water. Water can suffocate or extinguish the flame of a luckdragon because these creatures are always inhaling air.

● Falkor understands the language of water because all the languages of joy are closely related.

Norwegian Ridgeback

WINGS
Leathery wings allow the dragon to circle the skies, hunting and swooping down on its prey in a surprise attack.

CLAWS
Curved, razor-sharp talons give the dragon a firm, deadly grip as it bears its prey away to kill and devour it in a secluded location.

BODY
At birth, the scales covering its body are thin and soft. As the dragon matures, they harden into thick plates.

HEAD
Bronze horns are used to fight other dragons. During courtship, males use their horns to strip trees of bark to impress females.

JAWS
The dragon uses its muscular jaws lined with venomous fangs to kill and eat water-dwelling creatures and large mammals.

Hagrid, keeper of the keys and grounds at Hogwarts, keeps a baby Norwegian Ridgeback named Norbert as a pet in J.K. Rowling's *Harry Potter and the Sorcerer's Stone.* Hagrid wins the black dragon egg from a stranger during a card game and secretly brings it back to Hogwarts. He hatches the egg by placing it in the center of a fire. Within one week Norbert is three times his original size and smoke is issuing from his nostrils. Norbert sneezes sparks, a sign he will soon develop into a full-fledged fire-breather. The Norwegian Ridgeback can breathe fire at one to three months old, earlier than any other breed.

6 ft
(1.8 m)

SIZE COMPARISON

▶ ACCORDING TO *Fantastic Beasts and Where to Find Them* by Newt Scamander, a required text at Hogwarts School, the Norwegian Ridgeback is extremely aggressive to its own kind, making it a rare dragon. Legend states that one carried away and devoured a baby whale off the coast of Norway in 1802. Norbert is a hazard in captivity. His tail banging against the wall rattles windows, and wounds from the bite of his venomous fangs turn green. Hagrid must feed Norbert dead rats by the crateful to satisfy his ravenous appetite.

Where in the world?

● NORWAY

The Norwegian Ridgeback originated in the Norwegian mountains, where it eats water-dwelling creatures and singes the landscape regularly. There have also been sightings at Hogwarts in Britain and in Romania.

Did you know?

● According to Headmaster Dumbledore, one of the twelve uses of dragon's blood is as an oven cleaner.

● The Warlock's Convention of 1709 outlawed dragon breeding. It is illegal to keep a dragon as a pet in the wizarding world.

● Dragon eggs are considered Class A Non-Tradable Goods.

● Hatchlings should be fed a bucket of chicken-blood-and-brandy mixture.

● Despite Hagrid's good intentions, Norwegian Ridgebacks are impossible to train or domesticate.

● It is especially unwise to keep a fire-breathing dragon as a pet if you live in a wooden house.

Chrysophylax Dives *(krih-SOH-fy-laks DY-vees)*

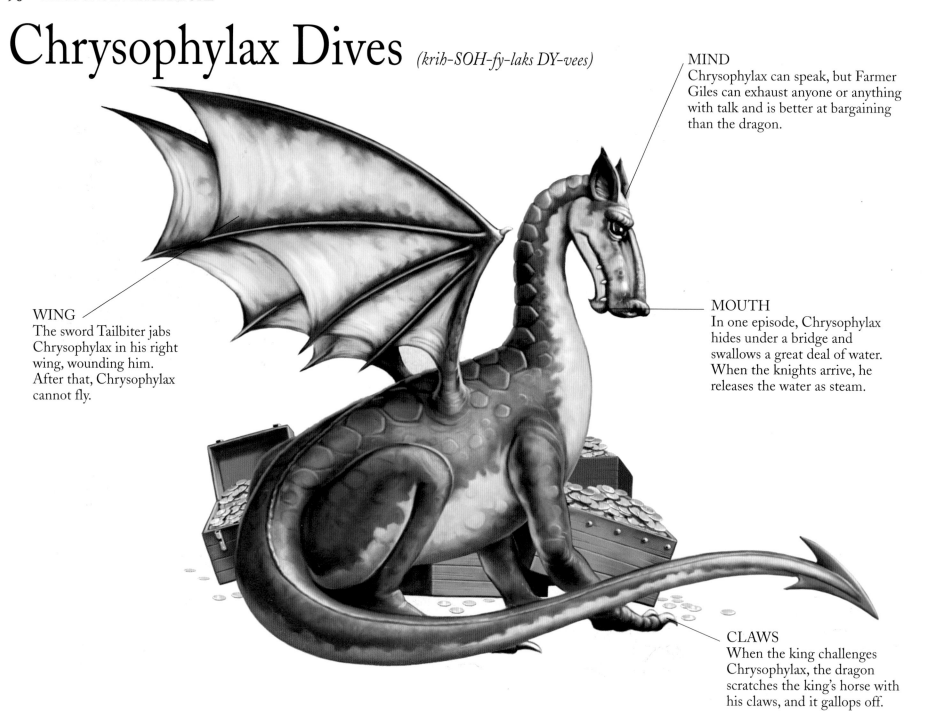

MIND
Chrysophylax can speak, but Farmer Giles can exhaust anyone or anything with talk and is better at bargaining than the dragon.

WING
The sword Tailbiter jabs Chrysophylax in his right wing, wounding him. After that, Chrysophylax cannot fly.

MOUTH
In one episode, Chrysophylax hides under a bridge and swallows a great deal of water. When the knights arrive, he releases the water as steam.

CLAWS
When the king challenges Chrysophylax, the dragon scratches the king's horse with his claws, and it gallops off.

I n *Father Giles of Ham*, not only has it been so long since knights have seen dragons that they have begun to think dragons do not exist, but it has been so long since dragons have seen knights that they have begun to wonder if knights exist. Then, the dragon Chrysophylax begins eating farm animals and people in the kingdom.

6 ft
(1.8 m)

SIZE COMPARISON

The king, having heard that Farmer Giles once defeated a giant, sends him to slay the dragon. Giles does not want to go. He is a farmer, not a knight, and it is a dangerous mission. He does not think he is a hero and is not interested in trying to become one.

▶ WITH HIS TALKING DOG GARM, HIS MARE, AND HIS MAGIC SWORD TAILBITER, Farmer Giles sets off to find the dragon. When his horse sees the dragon, it collapses in fear, and Giles falls off its back. However, Tailbiter acts with a mind of its own and stabs Chrysophylax in its wing. Now, Chrysophylax cannot fly away. He talks to Farmer Giles. When he tries to run away, Giles chases the dragon on his horse. Unable to escape, Chrysophylax is led to the village by Farmer Giles. But when Chrysophylax promises to bring the people many riches if they set him free, they foolishly believe him.

Where in the world?

GREAT
BRITAIN

The story of *Farmer Giles of Ham* is set near the River Thames in the fictitious "Little Kingdom" in Great Britain many centuries ago. The events probably take place near Oxford, where Tolkien lived.

Did you know?

● Chrysophylax does not keep his promise to return with riches for the villagers, so Farmer Giles and knights are sent to find him. The other knights flee when Chrysophylax swoops down on them, but Farmer Giles, his mare, and Tailbiter do not let Chrysophylax get away.

● *Farmer Giles of Ham* was written by J. R. R. Tolkien and published in 1949. Tolkien is also the author of *The Hobbit*, *The Lord of the Rings*, and *The Silmarillion*.

● The name Chrysophylax Dives is created from Latin and Greek. Chrysophylax is Greek for "gold-guard" and Dives is Latin for "rich."

● Years later, Chrysophylax returns to his cave to find another dragon has set up home there. Chrysophylax eats him.

Green Death

EARS
Green Death has excellent hearing, which it uses to sense predators or possible victims.

EYES
With six eyes, Green Death does not have a blind spot; it can see in all directions.

NOSE
Green Death uses its well-developed sense of smell to hunt down its victims.

TAIL
Sea dragons have many similarities to dinosaurs. They have a head like a Tyrannosaurus rex, thick legs like sauropods, and a clubbed tail like an ankylosaurus.

BREATH
It can breathe enough fire at one time to set alight an entire fleet of Viking ships. However, it is hard to control the fire inside its belly, and this can set its whole body alight.

Green Death is the main dragon villain in the novel and film *How To Train Your Dragon*. Hiccup is a Viking boy who is about to be exiled because he has failed to train his pet dragon. Green Death arrives on Hiccup's island. Hiccup, being the only one who can speak Dragonese, is sent to find out if the dragon comes in peace or to wage war. Green Death explains that it has come in peace but that it will still eat Hiccup later on. To avoid being eaten, Hiccup and his friends plan to kill Green Death by tricking another dragon, Purple Death, into helping them.

6 ft
(1.8 m)

SIZE COMPARISON

▶ IN THE BATTLE WITH GREEN DEATH, Purple Death is killed and Green Death is wounded. This makes the dragon so angry that he gobbles up Hiccup. Fortunately, Hiccup is caught on a Roman spear lodged in Green Death's throat and is not completely swallowed. Inside Green Death, Hiccup discovers the fire holes that create the dragon's flames. Taking his Viking helmet, Hiccup blocks Green Death's fire holes. When Green Death tries to burn Hiccup's father, the fire cannot be released, and instead Green Death is blown up. Having defeated the dragon, Hiccup is now a hero and is not exiled.

Where in the world?

SCANDINAVIA

The *How To Train Your Dragon* stories are set in a fictitious Viking world, somewhere in Scandinavia.

Did you know?

● Between 2003 and 2012, twelve *How To Train Your Dragon* novels were published. Cressida Cowell wrote them.

● In the film *How To Train Your Dragon*, the character Green Death was changed to Red Death.

● Green Death is a Seadragonus Giganticus Maximus. These "preposterously huge" fire-breathing dragons are many times the size of a Tyrannosaurus rex. In Viking mythology, they are the biggest dragon species and can easily crush a Viking's house.

● Hiccup has two pet dragons: hunting dragon Toothless and flying dragon Windwalker. Toothless helps rescue Hiccup from Green Death.

● Hiccup is unlike other Vikings because he is not strong and he is thin. However, he is very intelligent.

Smaug

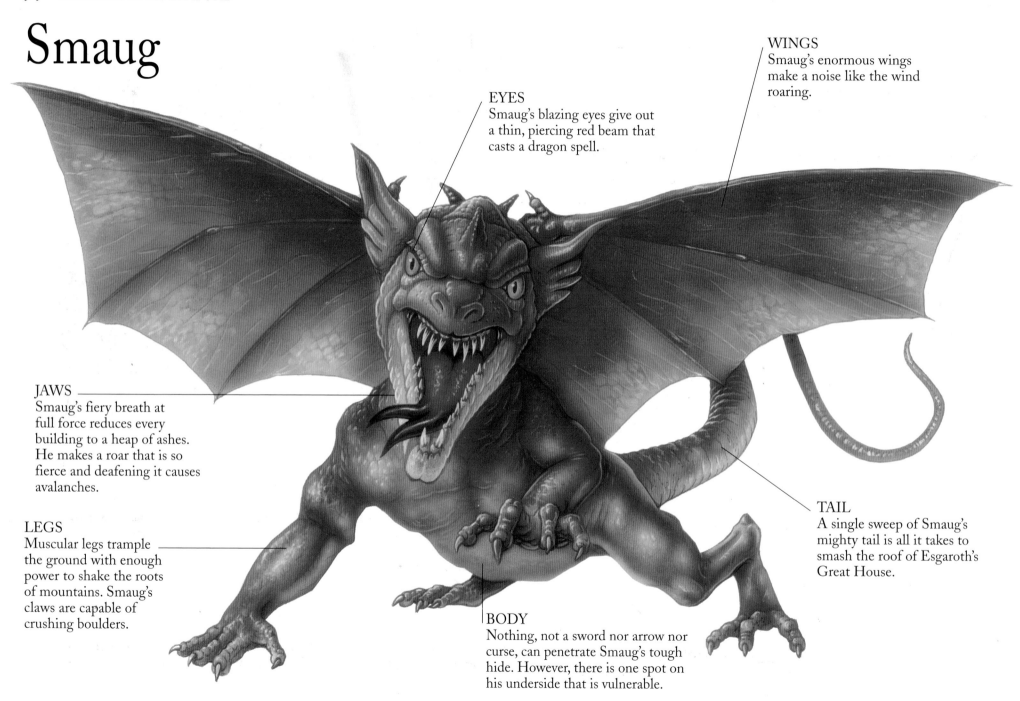

WINGS
Smaug's enormous wings make a noise like the wind roaring.

EYES
Smaug's blazing eyes give out a thin, piercing red beam that casts a dragon spell.

JAWS
Smaug's fiery breath at full force reduces every building to a heap of ashes. He makes a roar that is so fierce and deafening it causes avalanches.

LEGS
Muscular legs trample the ground with enough power to shake the roots of mountains. Smaug's claws are capable of crushing boulders.

TAIL
A single sweep of Smaug's mighty tail is all it takes to smash the roof of Esgaroth's Great House.

BODY
Nothing, not a sword nor arrow nor curse, can penetrate Smaug's tough hide. However, there is one spot on his underside that is vulnerable.

Isolated deep within the Lonely Mountain, Smaug the Golden sleeps atop the pile of treasure that he stole from the dwarves. Smaug makes his bed on the mass of ornaments, utensils, weapons, and gems that he hoards. He lies upon the gems for so long that they stick to his soft belly, forming a dazzling protective armor. At the end of a hot tunnel in a dungeon hall dug by dwarves, Smaug's gurgling snore can be heard. His lair gives off an eerie red glow and wisps of vapor. Although one of Smaug's drooping eyelids stays open enough to watch for thieves, Bilbo the hobbit is able to sneak in and steal a two-handled cup from the treasure hoard.

6 ft
(1.8 m)

SIZE COMPARISON

▶ THE DISCOVERY OF THIS THEFT INFURIATES SMAUG. He circles the sky above the mountain in a rage, bellowing and shooting flames. Later, Bilbo makes himself invisible and sneaks into the dragon's cave again. Although Smaug cannot see Bilbo, he can smell him and he mocks the invisible hobbit. Bilbo flatters the vain Smaug into rolling over onto his back. Bilbo spots an open patch in Smaug's jeweled armor. Knowledge of his weak spot is passed on to Bard the Bowman, who kills Smaug with a single, black, dwarf-made arrow.

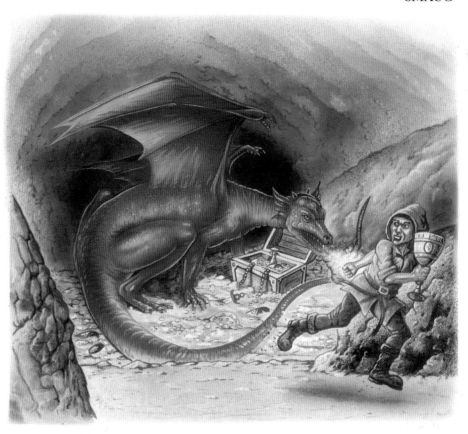

Where in the world?

Smaug is the last of the great dragons of Middle Earth in J.R.R. Tolkien's *The Hobbit*. His lair is deep within the Lonely Mountain.

● LONELY MOUNTAIN

Middle Earth

Did you know?

● It is unwise to reveal one's true name to a dragon.

● Many experts believe that a dragon is able to breathe fire because it stores a mixture of gases in its body. These gases ignite upon contact with the air, producing an intense flame.

● The dragon's ability to store gases such as methane may account for its terrible stench.

● There is no record of any dragon dying of old age. All dragons in recorded history have died from accidents, disease, or battle injuries.

● Dragons have heightened senses of smell, sight, and hearing. Some breeds can see objects as far as a mile (1.6 km) away and hear sounds well out of the range of the human ear.

Index